T0044060

Positively

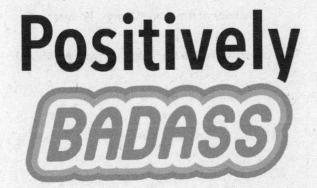

Other books by Becca Anderson

Badass Affirmations

The Book of Awesome Women

The Book of Awesome Girls

The Book of Awesome Women Writers

The Book of Awesome Black Women (with MJ Fievre)

You Are an Awesome Woman

Badass Advice

New Beginnings

Positively

Affirmations and Words of Positivity for Empowered Women

Becca Anderson

CORAL GABLES

Cover Design: Elina Diaz
Cover Photo/illustration: InnaPoka/stock.adobe.com
Layout & Design: Elina Diaz

For permission requests, please contact the publisher at:
Mango Publishing Group
2850 S Douglas Road, 4th Floor
Coral Gables, FL 33134 USA
info@mango.bz

For special orders, quantity sales, course adoptions and corporate sales, please email the publisher at sales@mango.bz. For trade and wholesale sales, please contact Ingram Publisher Services at customer.service@ingramcontent.com or +1.800.509.4887.

Positively Badass: Affirmations and Words of Positivity for Empowered Women

Library of Congress Cataloging-in-Publication number: 2022940949
ISBN: (print) 978-1-68481-001-7 (eBook) 978-1-68481-002-4
BISAC category code SEL004000, SELF-HELP / Affirmations

To the badass women in my life. Friends, family, and everything in between—thank you for always inspiring me to do and be better.

Table of Contents

INTRODUCTION

Like its predecessor *Badass Affirmations,* this book highlights badass women. It also brings to light the many issues we face as women—now that we are armed with amazing affirmations, when times are tough and we begin to doubt ourselves, we must turn the negatives into positives: hence the title *Positively Badass.*

As women, we are nearly constantly faced with the challenge of negative thoughts and feelings: worrying about how we look, or about things we said (or should have said) and how we are perceived in arenas like the workplace. Many women are naturally confident in themselves and do not let this kind of thinking in. I applaud you! But many others do have trouble coping with the day-to-day struggle of being a woman in this world.

This book is for both of these types of ladies. Whether you are completely comfortable with who you are (again, kudos) or anxious beyond measure about your everyday existence, you will discover tidbits of truth in the pages to come that will apply to you. Positivity is a key ingredient to life. When we speak encouraging words to ourselves, it gives us the drive to be courageous. For thousands of years, women were kept in the background, unable to speak their minds, overlooked and underestimated. Today, women are achieving more than ever before (although society is still catching up), and with this freedom we hold, we can do whatever it is we aspire to do—and positive thinking along the way is a surefire way to make it to the finish line.

But it's not just about being positive. We need to take it a step further than that. In addition, we as women need to remember to take care of ourselves, which manifests itself in a number of different ways: self-care, setting boundaries, having a solid support system; the list goes on. Being a woman is overwhelming—there is no question about that. But the good news is that we are here to help take some of that worry off your shoulders with healthy practices for everyday life.

This book highlights all the many and varied ways to go about living your best badass life. Read on for thought-provoking stories, inspiring quotations, and supportive reinforcement that will take you down the road toward becoming positively badass.

Chapter 1

EXPRESS YOURSELF (AND DON'T HOLD BACK)

Strut Your Stuff

You embody your own style. This may be an obvious observation, but often we find ourselves comparing what we see in the mirror to the women we see in magazines, on television or film, or even in our everyday lives. What we don't see is what happens when the camera clicks off. Many of these women dress or portray themselves in a certain way that is not necessarily who they are, and imitating that should not be something we emulate when we already have our own essence.

Our styles tend to shift and evolve throughout our lives, particularly when we go through major changes. A close friend of mine purchases an outlandish item when something drastic happens—a job is lost, a relationship comes to an end, etc. She uses it as sort of a reverse good luck charm, but I believe it is her way of embracing her beauty on her own terms. And let's point out the obvious: Sometimes buying something that allows us to completely reinvent ourselves (which doesn't have to break the bank) is a beautiful and healthy way to not only accessorize but expand our lives.

Affirmation Station

I am not going to compare myself to anyone else.
I choose to wear things that are true to me.
I will let my own unique style shine.

Weird Is the New Awesome

We are often told that we must look, act, and feel certain ways to be perceived as appealing. If you want to be seen as beautiful, you must wear these clothes, have this hair, or even switch out glasses for contacts. And it is not limited to looks, this concept extends to our personalities as well. Labels such as the "loud girl," the "quirky girl," or the "shy girl" are often placed on us without hesitation. If a woman struggles with her sense of self-worth or has alternative hobbies or interests, she is viewed as "strange." In almost every romantic comedy ever made, the leading lady is a confident, attractive woman who gets the guy, while her kooky sidekick sits in the background cheering her on. This is not a snapshot to be manifested and placed into your reality.

Affirmation Station

I am my own person.
I can try new things.
I will always celebrate myself.

The Best Version of You Is...You!

Every outfit you admire, every color that lights up your face, every pair of shoes you flip for—they all reflect you at your best, ready to take on the world. No matter what type of woman you are—hipster, supermodel, academic—you are absolutely correct. There is no right way to be. How you choose to show yourself to the world and what makes you truly happy as a human being is how you should be living your life every single day without hesitation.

Affirmation Station

I will express myself honestly.
I am never wrong in how I choose to be.
I love every part of me.

No Labels Allowed

No one should make you feel ashamed of the things that make you happy. If you have been pigeonholed by one of these labels—let's, say you are an athlete and love playing sports but decide to learn how to play a musical instrument and join a band—this is something you must keep in mind. Labels should not limit us from doing the things that we love. If you grew up interested in certain things but those interests shifted later in life, that is A-OK. As Marianne Williamson put it so well, "Our deepest fear is not that we are inadequate. Our deepest fear is that we are powerful beyond measure." Know yourself, and don't hold back. Give yourself permission to find the best within you and let it shine without shame or apology. Nobody's going to benefit from your hesitation—you've got too much to get done to keep your talents hidden away just so that others are more comfortable around you. Dare to be powerful. Try it out.

All those clichés—roll with the punches, just do it, you'll never know until you try, you can do anything you set your mind to—well, they get stuck in our heads because they're true. So go for it!

Block Out the Noise

1. If you're thinking of trying out a new style, give it a go for a week. If it doesn't feel like you, simply go back to what feels right. There is nothing wrong with stepping outside one's everyday expression zone.

2. Always feel comfortable. Don't wear high heels just because you feel you should. If there is an occasion that calls for fancy footwear, find something that suits both you and your surroundings.

3. Never let anyone tell you your style is wrong. Love bellbottoms? Rock 'em and never apologize.

"You just have to look past it. You look how you look, be comfortable."

—Jennifer Lawrence, Oscar-winning actress known for her candid and honest personality

"Don't think about making women fit the world—think about making the world fit women."

—Gloria Steinem, feminist journalist and social political activist who stood as a leader and a spokeswoman for the American feminist movement of the 1960s and '70s

"I think your whole life shows in your face, and you should be proud of that."

—Lauren Bacall, classic Hollywood actress known for her wide-minded views

"It's a tiny revolution to express yourself fully and be who you want to be, especially when systems tell you that you can't. I've realized how powerful it is for me to just discuss with young people and begin conversations."

—Amandla Stenberg, performer and singer included in *TIME*'s list of Most Influential Teens in both 2015 and 2016

Affirmation Station

I am comfortable with who I am.

I will never apologize for being myself.

I can be whoever I want to be.

"When I am putting looks together, I dare myself to make something work. I always look for the most interesting silhouette or something that's a little off, but I have to figure it out. I have to make it me. I think that's the thrill in fashion."

—Rihanna, singer, actress, and fashion designer who has sold over 250 million records

"Don't adjust your self-expression to find an audience. You will regret it. It's only fun if you are accepted as you are. And you will be, one day."

—Yoko Ono, world-famous artist and musician who has influenced millions

"Toughness doesn't have to come in a pinstripe suit."

—Dianne Feinstein, politician and US Senator for the state of California since 1992

"In the last year or two, I've become more confident and more comfortable. I never set out to be a clothing designer—I was an uncomfortable person, and so I wanted comfortable clothes. Women have great power—our voices and decisions can make a huge difference in the world."

—Eileen Fisher, fashion designer and entrepreneur who founded the clothing brand Eileen Fisher Inc.

Affirmation Station

My style is my own.
I will smile when I look in the mirror.
I will always encourage myself.

"Style is based on who you are."

–Isabella Rossellini, actress, author, philanthropist, and model

"There is no cosmetic for beauty like happiness."

–Maria Mitchell, astronomer, librarian, naturalist, and educator

"To lose confidence in one's body is to lose confidence in oneself."

–Simone de Beauvoir, writer, existentialist philosopher, political activist, and social theorist who played a big part in the development of feminism

Simone de Beauvoir

Existentialist writer Simone de Beauvoir was the founder of the feminist movement in France. Her book *The Second*

Sex immediately took a place of importance in the feminist
canon upon its publication in 1949, establishing de Beauvoir's
reputation as a first-rate thinker. Although her brutally honest
examination of the condition of women in the first half of the
twentieth century shocked some delicate sensibilities, others
were gratified to have someone tell the truth of women's
experience as "relative beings."

Born in 1908 to what she characterized as "bourgeois" parents,
she met the philosopher Jean-Paul Sartre in her early twenties
in a salon study group at Paris's famed university, the Sorbonne.
They recognized each other as soulmates immediately and
stayed together for fifty-one years in a highly unorthodox
partnership, wherein they left openings for "contingent loves"
so as not to limit their capacity for enriching experiences. She
eschewed motherhood and all forms of domesticity; the duo
preferred cafés for all their meals. They lived together only very
briefly during World War II and had difficulty protecting their
privacy as word of the trendy new philosophy they espoused
spread and their international prestige heightened.

While Sartre is generally credited as the creator of
existentialism, de Beauvoir and the circle of leftist intellectuals
that surrounded them were intricately involved in defining
the movement. Her treatise *Existentialism and the Wisdom of
the Ages* postulates the human condition as neutral, neither

inherently good nor evil: "[The individual] is nothing at first," she theorized; "it is up to him to make himself good or bad depending upon whether he assumes his freedom or denies it." De Beauvoir's first literary efforts were fictional. In 1943's *She Came to Stay*, she fictionalizes the story of Sartre's youthful protégé Olga Kosakiewicz, who entered into a triangular living relationship with the two French intellectuals. Next, she tackled the male point of view in her epic treatment of death, *All Men Are Mortal*, a novel whose central character was an immortal she tracked for seven centuries. In 1954, after the success of *The Second Sex*, de Beauvoir returned to fiction with *The Mandarins*, a novelization of the splintered and disenchanted French intelligentsia which included thinly disguised portrayals of Sartre, Albert Camus, and Nelson Algren, among others, and went on to win the Illustrious Goncourt Prize.

She continued to write and publish, creating a weighty body of work. Her penetrating mind is perhaps most evident in the series of five memoirs she wrote, the most famous of which is the first, *Memoirs of a Dutiful Daughter*. She outlived Sartre and died on a Paris summer day in 1986 after a long and thoughtful life, leaving a legacy of significant contributions to gender and identity issues as well as to philosophy and literature.

"You are your best thing."

—Toni Morrison, prolific novelist who won countless awards for her literary works

"Throw yourself to the edge that you're always scared of. Try being independent; do it your way. You'll love it."

—Ameerah Al-Taweel, philanthropist, humanitarian, and former Saudi Arabian princess

---

Affirmation Station

I will not be subject to stereotypes.

I love the person I am.

Everything about me is beautiful, inside and out.

Ella Fitzgerald

Known as the "First Lady of Song," Ella Fitzgerald was a bona fide legend and one of the most influential vocalists in the music industry, with a career that spanned over six decades.

Fitzgerald was born on April 25, 1917, to a troubled household in Virginia. She soon moved to New York with her mother, who left her father behind. As the family grew, Fitzgerald worked odd jobs to make ends meet, but soon found herself living on the street, all the while hoping to make it as an entertainer. She decided to make these dreams a reality and entered a contest at Harlem's Apollo Theater, singing and wowing the crowd. Fun fact: She originally wanted to be a dancer but panicked and decided to sing instead. This happy accident won Fitzgerald first place; little did she know this would kickstart her legendary career as a jazz artist.

She began singing regularly at jazz clubs, then recorded the tune "Love and Kisses" with Chick Webb (who had become her guardian when Fitzgerald's mother passed away) and eventually joined his band. In 1938, she put out her first number one hit, "A-Tisket, A-Tasket." She also began performing with the Benny Goodman Orchestra and developed her own side project, Ella Fitzgerald and the Savoy Eight.

In the early 1940s, Fitzgerald landed her own record deal and made her film debut in the comedy western *Ride 'Em Cowboy* with Bud Abbott and Lou Costello. She continued to perform and started Jazz at the Philharmonic, a series of concerts and live records with other performers. She also went on tour with

Dizzy Gillespie and his band, where she began to change up her smooth singing with scat stylings.

Fitzgerald earned her title of "First Lady of Song" as she continued to soar in popularity throughout the 1950s and '60s and won her first two Grammy awards—the first African American woman to do so. She collaborated with music legends Louis Armstrong, Count Basie, and Frank Sinatra.

She began to suffer serious health issues later in life, losing both her legs to diabetes in 1993 and eventually passing away in 1996. By that time, she had recorded nearly 2,000 songs and won fourteen Grammys, including one for lifetime achievement, and was also awarded the Presidential Medal of Freedom.

> *"Women are the real architects of society."*
>
> —Cher, actress, singer, and television personality who has been called the "Goddess of Pop" and has sold over 100 million records

> *"In a world that wants women to whisper, I choose to yell."*
>
> —Luvvie Ajayi, bestselling author of *I'm Judging You: The Do-Better Manual*

Halet Çambel

How many people can say they dissed Hitler? Halet Çambel, an Olympic fencer, was the first Muslim woman ever to compete in the Olympics as well as an archaeologist.

She was born in 1916 in Berlin, Germany, the daughter of a former Grand Vizier to the Ottoman sultan. When her family moved back to Istanbul, Turkey, in the mid-1920s, Çambel was "shocked by the black-shrouded women who came and visited us at home." Having survived bouts with typhoid and hepatitis as a child, she decided to focus on exercise to build her strength and health. In an interview, she said, "There were other activities like folk dancing and other dances at school, but I chose fencing." Çambel eventually rose to the level of representing Turkey in the women's individual foil event at the 1936 Summer Olympics. The twenty-year-old had grave reservations about attending the Nazi-run Games, and she and her fellow Turkish athletes drew the line at a social introduction to the Führer; late in life, she recalled, "Our assigned German official asked us to meet Hitler. We actually would not have come to Germany at all if it were down to us, as we did not approve of Hitler's regime. We firmly rejected her offer."

Upon returning home after the Games, Çambel met communist poet and journalist Nail Çakırhan and fell in love. Her family didn't approve of his Marxist ideas, so they were married in secret; their marriage endured for seventy years, until his death in 2008. She studied archaeology in Paris at the Sorbonne in the 1930s before earning a doctorate at Istanbul University in 1944, then became a lecturer in 1947. That same year, she worked as part of a team excavating the eighth century Hittite fortress city of Kartepe in Turkey, which was to become her scholarly life's work. She spent half of each year there for the next fifty years, working with others to achieve a deeper understanding of Hittite hieroglyphic writing and other aspects of their culture.

In 1960, Çambel became a professor of Prehistoric Archaeology at Istanbul University and founded its Institute of Prehistory, achieving emeritus status in 1984. She lived to be ninety-seven.

"Once you figure out who you are and what you love about yourself, I think it all kind of falls into place."

—Jennifer Aniston, actress and producer who has found incredible success in both television and film

"Why change? Everyone has their own style. When you have found it, you should stick to it."

—Audrey Hepburn, actress and humanitarian famous for her award-winning performances in film and on stage

"Give a girl the right shoes and she can conquer the world."

–Marilyn Monroe, actress and performer famous for her roles as a "blonde bombshell," remembered also as an icon of the '60s sexual revolution

"When a woman says, 'I have nothing to wear!' what she really means is, 'There's nothing here for who I'm supposed to be today.' "

–Caitlin Moran, journalist and author of the bestselling novel *How to Build a Girl* and its sequels

Affirmation Station

I choose to accept myself.

I will never conform.

I will always love the person I chose to be.

"Fashion can be bought. Style one must possess."

—Edna Woolman Chase, fashion leader and icon who served as the Editor-in-Chief of *Vogue* for over forty years

"I base my fashion sense on what doesn't itch."

—Gilda Radner, actress, comedian, and performer on the popular television comedy show *Saturday Night Live*

"The only rule is don't be boring...Life is too short to blend in."

—Paris Hilton, actress, media personality, socialite, businesswoman, model, singer, DJ, and heiress to the Hilton hotel empire

"No matter what it is you want to do in life, it's important to be yourself."

–Aubrey Anderson Emmons, child actress who starred in the award-winning sitcom *Modern Family*

Affirmation Station

I will wear whatever makes me smile.

I am awesomely unique.

I can express myself however I choose.

"Stop telling girls they can be anything they want when they grow up. I think it's a mistake. Not because they can't, but because it would have never occurred to them that they couldn't."

–Sarah Silverman, stand-up comedian, actress, and writer, known for her straightforward and unapologetic humor

"Everybody needs a passion. That's what keeps life interesting. If you live without passion, you can go through life without leaving any footprints."

–Betty White, quoted from her book *If You Ask Me (And Of Course You Won't)*, actress and comedian often called "The First Lady of Television"

"A woman with a voice is by definition a strong woman. But the search to find that voice can be remarkably difficult."

–Melinda French Gates, philanthropist who has been consistently ranked by *Forbes* as one of the most powerful women in the world

"Even if it makes others uncomfortable, I love who I am."

–Janelle Monáe, actor, singer, and rapper nominated for eight Grammys

---

Affirmation Station

I will always be honest in what I wear, say, and do.
I decide who and what I will be no matter what others think.
I choose to show my true self always.

"I leave you. I leave you hope...I leave you racial dignity."

–Mary McLeod Bethune, educator, philanthropist,
humanitarian, and civil rights activist

Mary McLeod Bethune

In 1904, Mary McLeod Bethune started a school with $1.50
and a dream situated on the grounds of a former dump site.
"I haunted the city dump retrieving discarded linen and
kitchenware, cracked dishes, broken chairs, pieces of old
lumber," she remembered later. From this humble beginning,
it has now blossomed into Bethune Cookman College in
Daytona, Florida.

Hard work was never something that daunted her; she was used
to picking 250 pounds of cotton a day and pulling the plow

when the family mule died. The fifteenth of seventeen children born to former slaves, Bethune was brought up as a strict Methodist and taught to believe in the sweat of the brow and faith in God. At the age of twelve, she was given a scholarship by the Quakers to be educated at an integrated school in North Carolina, later going on to Moody Bible College. Coming from these experiences, she had a profound respect for education, particularly for its value in helping her people rise from poverty.

Bethune's school succeeded through her combination of penny-pinching abilities and excellent fundraising skills—she even got J.D. Rockefeller to contribute. She trained the students to pick elderberries to make into ink, used charcoal made of burned wood for chalk, and bartered free tuition for food for her students. Soon she added an infirmary on the site when she realized Black people couldn't get medical treatment within 200 miles of that part of the Atlantic Coast; eventually, that infirmary grew into a training hospital for doctors and nurses. By 1922, the school boasted 300 students; Bethune stayed on as president of the college until 1942.

She had a strong commitment to African Americans, particularly women. While running the school, she led the campaign to register Black women voters despite threats from the KKK. Her civil rights activism and humanitarianism brought her into contact with many people, including Eleanor Roosevelt, with whom she became good friends. Bethune ended up serving people in many leadership roles, including as the founder and president of the National Council of Negro Women, the leading member of the "Black Cabinet," who were advisors to FDR on African American needs and interests, and the Director of the Office of Minority Affairs of the National Youth Administration. When she was seventy-seven, concerned over the inability of Black people to get life insurance, she started the Central Life Insurance Company, becoming the only woman president of a national life insurance company in the entire United States.

For these and other accomplishments, Mary McLeod Bethune was regarded as the most influential Black woman in America until her death in 1955. Bethune's rise from poverty to national leadership is sheer sheroism.

"Bring your whole self to the experience. Because the more we do that, the more that people get to see that, the more comfortable everybody's gonna be with it."

—Bozoma Saint John, businesswoman and marketing executive who holds the title of Chief Marketing Officer for streaming giant Netflix

"I'm gonna make what I want to make, and other people are gonna like what they're gonna like. It doesn't really matter."

—Billie Eilish, Grammy Award-winning singer and songwriter

Affirmation Station

I approve of myself.

I love myself deeply and fully.

My life is a gift.

"I have chosen to no longer be apologetic for my femaleness and my femininity. And I want to be respected in all of my femaleness because I deserve to be."

—Chimamanda Ngozi Adichie, writer whose works include novels, short stories, and nonfiction

"I taught myself confidence. When I'd walk into a room and feel scared to death, I'd tell myself, 'I'm not afraid of anybody.' And people believed me. You've got to teach yourself to take over the world."

—Priyanka Chopra, actress, singer, and film producer who has received numerous accolades including a National Film Award and five Filmfare Awards

"We grew up in a time with every single one of our moves being recorded and documented forever, and in that was this idea that we can't make mistakes, but when that's not happening, you're also not growing."

—Rupi Kaur, poet, illustrator, photographer, and author who rose to prominence on Instagram, eventually becoming one of the most popular "Instapoets"

"Always be a first-rate version of yourself, instead of a second-rate version of somebody else."

—Judy Garland, actress and singer who had a career that spanned forty-five years both on film and the stage

"I am made and remade continually. Different people draw different words from me."

—Virginia Woolf, writer who is considered one of the most important modernist authors of the twentieth century

---

Affirmation Station

I tell my own story.
I will choose what I show to the world.
I am able to free myself from fear.

"The worst walls are never the ones you find in your way. The worst walls are the ones you put there."

—Ursula K. Le Guin, celebrated author of published works that include novels, short stories, poetry, and essays, winning her several literary awards

"I just love bossy women. I could be around them all day. To me, bossy is not a pejorative term at all. It means somebody's passionate and engaged and ambitious and doesn't mind leading..."

—Amy Poehler, comedic actress famous for her television performances on *Saturday Night Live* and *Parks and Recreation*, and later for her memoir *Yes Please*

"The worst enemy to creativity is self-doubt."

—Sylvia Plath, poet and novelist best known for her classic work *The Bell Jar*

"I just try to be myself. I hope I encourage people just to be themselves, no matter what happens."

—Mo'ne Davis, former Little League Baseball pitcher and current Hampton University softball player who was the first African American girl to play in the Little League and the first girl ever to pitch a shutout and earn a win at the Little League World Series

Take Me As I Am

We as humans evolve and change; this is normal and expected of us. This doesn't just apply to our clothing and accessory style—expression encompasses all of the ways we show ourselves to the world. The so-called labels others tag us with are nothing more than stickers meant to be ripped off and thrown away. You are not simply one type of woman. Many of us are multi-faceted: Maybe Monday through Friday you are a lawyer, but you take ballet classes on the weekends. Perhaps you struggle with dyslexia, yet you are taking an online workshop to overcome this and write the novel you always dreamed of writing. Do it! Some of the most unexpected people have achieved their self-realization goals. Even more so, if you are someone who is stepping out of your comfort zone and into a new environment despite others' judgments, you can be one of the most valuable and important voices in that room. You are someone who can provide fresh takes, new perspectives, and perhaps a better way of doing things that others have not yet considered.

Madonna said it herself: Express Yourself. While part of the tune references getting a man to open up about his feelings (a near impossible task if there ever was one), the larger message more deeply applies to life. We should never go for second best. We should never settle. Do not wear something just because you feel like you can't pull off the style you truly want to rock. You should never be afraid of changing something about yourself because you feel inspired. And most importantly, you should never be afraid to speak your mind and make your voice heard. Just make sure to do it in your favorite pair of shoes.

Chapter 2

LOVING YOUR BODY

Turn Insecurity into Inspiration

Contrary to what the media tells us, no one has "the"
perfect body. Before you can learn to love your body, you
need to relinquish the idea that you must fit the mold that
the world pushes on you every single day. The body of a woman
manifests in varying sizes, tones, and rhythms. You can totally
love your body in whatever phase it is in. Whether you have a
few extra pounds or you can't seem to gain weight, no matter
what you look like, you are beautiful. The key is not to compare
yourself to others and how they look! It is a silly endeavor to
look at others and wish we could look or act like them. While it's
an impossibility, it is also an injustice to who you are as a human.

If you see yourself as average or less than, know that you
possess unique characteristics that no one else can claim.
There is only one you. While you may not have made full
self-discovery yet, you will bring something to the table
that no one else can at many times throughout
your life. Whether you chose to find a partner,

get married, or stay single (and all of these choices are valid),
appreciation for who you are is essential to happiness. Loving
ourselves for every perfect flaw allows us the courage to take
chances in our lives and overcome obstacles.

Insecurity is something that affects all of us throughout our lives
in a multitude of ways. But it can inspire us to find greatness
within ourselves.

Affirmation Station

I am uniquely made.
I am full of positivity.
I see myself as beautiful.

Swap Out Comparison for Confidence

Your true power is in how you view yourself! So remind yourself
every day that you are beautiful and that you can do all of
the hard things set in front of you. Yes, those women on your
Instagram feed are beautiful, but hey, guess what? So are you!
Whether you believe it or not, somebody is looking at you like,

"Wow, I wish I had her legs…" or "Oh my, her arms are to die for!" Whether you have wrinkles or smooth skin, whether you look older or younger than actually are, there is something to be appreciated about you right now, exactly as you are!

Loving one's body can be challenging and complicated. It can even take some women to very dark places where they choose to go without proper nutrition to attain this supposedly perfect image. This thinking is dangerous and unhealthy. Change this perspective, remove yourself from that negative space, and view yourself the way that everyone else does: a gorgeous being with endless possibilities ahead of her.

Affirmation Station

I am free to live beautifully.
I am free from comparisons of the past.
I don't need to change to be seen as beautiful.

Moving Forward to Fabulous

Please remember that nobody stays the same size that they
were when they were in high school—so if you're one of those
that are constantly berating themselves over not being a size
four anymore, stop it. Life ebbs and flows, things change,
people come and go, and our weight is allowed to change
as well. Be kind to yourself, and know that it's okay to carry a
few more pounds than you did back in the day. The past is the
past for a reason. How you see yourself when you look in the
mirror should be totally different from how you saw yourself as
a teen. So for the health nuts out there, I'm not saying you aren't
allowed to go on a diet or try to lose weight—I just want you to
know that you're already beautiful right now. Yeah, you might
want certain parts of your body to be flatter or less wrinkly,
and that's great! It is totally okay to change something about
yourself if that is what you want, and if it is for you and no one
else. But you don't need those changes in order to be beautiful.
As long as you are living a healthy, fabulous life, you are doing
it right. Your body is a powerful instrument that is capable of
incredible things. Love it for the stunning specimen that is.

Decide now that you will stop telling yourself anything other
than the truth, and affirm that truth each and every day. Babe,
you're a beaut.

You Are the Fairest of Them All

Look in the mirror and tell yourself you are beautiful and intelligent three times a day for a month and see/feel your confidence grow.

"You are imperfect, permanently and inevitably flawed. And you are beautiful."

–Amy Bloom, writer and psychotherapist

"It's a healthy body that works every day, and I try hard not to judge it."

–Michelle Obama, author, attorney, activist, and wife of Barack Obama who has done advocacy work in many different sectors

"Celebrate yourself. Celebrate others. The things that make us different from one another make us beautiful."

–Ariana Grande, actress and singer with a four-octave vocal range

"I'd rather regret the risks that didn't work out than the chances I didn't take at all."

–Simone Biles, artistic gymnast who has won a combined total of thirty-two Olympic and World Championship medals

Simone Biles

Simone Biles, who was voted *TIME*'s Athlete of the Year in 2021,
made history by stepping down from the US team during the
2020 Tokyo Olympics.

Born in Columbus, Ohio in 1997, Biles was raised by her
grandparents, Ron and Nellie, after her mother proved to
be unfit to take care of Biles and her sister; the sisters were
eventually adopted by their grandparents, referring to Nellie as
"Mom." Biles became interested in gymnastics at an early age
and began to compete at only ten years old; by the year 2011,
she was at the junior elite level, taking the top spot in vault and
balance beam events. In 2013, she reached the senior elite
level in gymnastics, winning the US P&G Championships and
becoming the first African American female athlete to win gold
at the all-around in the World Championships. She continued
to win gold in vault, floor exercise, balance beam, and all-
around in competition. By 2015, she was considered one of
the country's top Olympic hopefuls, earning her spot on the US
team in 2016.

One of the shortest gymnasts to ever come across the Olympic
circuit, she stands tall at a height of four feet, eight inches.
However, Biles did not let her height become an obstacle. She
used her height and body to her advantage and became known

for her powerful tumbling in her floor routines. She also has a trick named after her: the Biles, and it consists of a double flip with legs straightened, ending with a half twist.

When competing in Tokyo, she began to struggle with her own well-being and knew that she could hurt herself and her team if she continued. Following this brave act, she was criticized and labeled a "quitter." This experience has made her an advocate for mental health—for making it acceptable to step back when things get difficult and take care of oneself. Biles later provided a testimony as a victim of Larry Nassar, a team doctor who sexually assaulted hundreds of young women in gymnastics.

Simone Biles stands as a role model for young women everywhere: You do have the power to take control of your mind and body. Her perseverance and dedication to pushing adversity out of the way has earned her the right to be one of the most decorated Olympians in history.

> *"You've got to be confident when you're competing. You've got to be a beast."*
>
> —Gabby Douglas, Olympic gymnast who is the first African American to have won the Olympic individual all-around title

"I think it's important for women and men to see and appreciate the beauty in their natural bodies."

—Beyoncé, actress, singer, philanthropist, and activist

"I realize everybody wants what they don't have. But at the end of the day, what you have inside is much more beautiful than what's on the outside!"

—Selena Gomez, actress and singer who is big on philanthropy and activism

---

Affirmation Station

I am responsible for taking care of me.

Loving myself feels good.

My well-being is the most important thing to me.

"You have to remember that the hard days are what make you stronger. The bad days make you realize what a good day is. If you never had any bad days, you would never have that sense of accomplishment!"

—Aly Raisman, artistic gymnast and two-time Olympian

"I think that women out there should just be happy with how they look and they shouldn't really try to conform to any stereotype. Just be happy and hopefully healthy."

–Rebel Wilson, actress and comedian well-known for starring in *Pitch Perfect*

"The same body you've had since you were a baby is the body you will inhabit when you are seventy-five years old."

–Cameron Diaz, actress, author, and environmental activist

"I'm never going to give up. They only shot a body, but they cannot shoot my dreams."

–Malala Yousafzai, Pakistani activist who survived a gunshot to the head and continues to spread advocacy and awareness from women's rights to education

"It's not what happens, it's how you deal with it."

–Tina Turner, singer and actress who is often referred to as "Queen of Rock 'n' Roll"

Affirmation Station

It's okay to love my body as it changes.

I want to treat my body with love and respect.

It's okay to love myself as I am now.

"You come into my world and you sit with me, my size, my hue, my age, and you…you sit, and you experience."

–Viola Davis, award-winning television and film actress and producer

"I'm wise enough by now to know that you're never going to please everyone so you may as well stop trying."

–Kelly Clarkson, singer, daytime talk-show host, and television personality known for winning the first season of *American Idol*

"Drink a bunch of water and get facials regularly. I take care of my skin."

–Angela Bassett, actress and producer known for playing diverse characters on screen and stage

"I'm not a trendsetter, I'm a singer. I'd rather weigh a ton and make an amazing album… My aim in life is never to be skinny."

–Adele, singer and songwriter who has done philanthropic work in several different countries

"I didn't understand why people couldn't accept me for who I was. … I'm not gonna conform and hurt myself and do something crazy to be a size two."

–Amber P. Riley, actress and singer most known for her six-year role on *Glee*

"If I wasn't confident in who I am or didn't like the fact that I was transgender, then I would not I have gotten as far as I have today."

–Jazz Jennings, YouTube personality, spokesmodel, television personality, and LGBTQIA+ rights activist

Affirmation Station

My body is worthy of love.

I can give love to my body.

I can trust the rhythm of my body.

"My great hope for us as young women is to start being kinder to ourselves so that we can be kinder to each other."

—Emma Stone, Oscar-winning actress

"I'm the lady next door when I'm not on stage."

—Aretha Franklin, singer and performer who won multiple Grammy awards and was the first female inductee to the Rock & Roll Hall of Fame

Helen Keller

Born in Tuscumbia, Alabama in 1880, Helen Keller was just nineteen months old when she was struck with an illness then known as "brain fever" that caused her body temperature to soar. After several days, her fever resided and all seemed normal, until her mother began noticing she did not react to sounds or anything in front of her. They soon realized the illness had both shut her eyes and closed her ears.

Throughout her childhood, she found small ways of communicating using signs, but was easily angered and frustrated, frequently throwing tantrums. While some of the family suggested she be institutionalized, her parents hired a teacher named Anne Sullivan to work with the little girl and teach her how to communicate effectively. Keller fought back and proved difficult until they moved the two of them to a small cottage where they could work together in a calmer environment. One of the first words Keller learned was "water," as Anne used the waterspout to demonstrate what the word meant and moved Keller's hands to show her how to spell the word. Using this technique, Keller learned how to spell out the names of the objects she touched. They would go on to work together for forty-nine years.

In 1890, Keller began attending a school for the deaf in Boston; she continued working toward her goal for twenty-five years of learning how to speak so that others would understand her. She would go on to attend college with her trusted mentor and friend Anne Sullivan. By then, she had mastered touch-lip reading, speech, Braille, typing, and finger-spelling. Keller graduated cum laude in 1904.

Keller was highly political, lobbying for the women's suffrage movement as well as labor rights and socialism, and standing up in opposition to military intervention. In her travels, she brought hope to many individuals with similar disabilities and motivated real change in the world as more opportunities and resources were provided for people who were visually impaired. She was an active member of the Industrial Workers of the World, as well as of the Socialist Party of America.

Despite all of the obstacles in her way, Helen Keller chose to push past her limitations and do great things with the life she was given. She will always be remembered as someone who did not let anything come between her and greatness.

"I wouldn't say I invented tacky, but I definitely brought it to its present high popularity."

—Bette Midler, singer, actress, and comedian with a career that spans over half a century

"I'm not offended by all the dumb blonde jokes because I know I'm not dumb. I also know I'm not blonde."

—Dolly Parton, actress, singer, and businesswoman who has founded and oversees several charity-focused organizations

"Nothing makes a woman more beautiful than the belief that she is beautiful."

—Sophia Loren, actress who grew up in poverty but turned her fortunes around

"This is who I am. I am proud at any size. And I love you and want you to be proud in any form you may take as well."

—Lady Gaga, singer and actress who wore a meat dress to the 2010 MTV Video Music Awards to comment on one's need to fight for what one believes in

"I'm not obsessed by how I look or with being reed thin, but I do think that as a woman in my fifties, I have forty years ahead. Looking after yourself goes hand in hand with looking good."

–Linda Evans, television star best known for her role as Krystle Carrington on the '80s hit series *Dynasty*

Affirmation Station

I take care of myself.
I am perfect in my imperfection.
I love every part of my body.

"We have to have faith in ourselves."

–Cynthia Heimel, humorist writer with a focus on feminism

"I represent the healthy, happy, curvy, strong woman. And that sounds much healthier to me than being eighty pounds and skinny as a bean."

–Heidi Klum, model, producer, and businesswoman

"You can only decide how you're going to live now."

–Joan Baez, musician and activist who made beautiful folk music that touched on social justice, energizing the political music scene of the sixties and seventies

"The kind of beauty I want most is the hard-to-get kind that comes from within: strength, courage, dignity."

—Ruby Dee, actress, playwright, and civil rights activist who during her lifetime used her presence on and off stage to talk about relevant issues

"You are all you will ever have for certain."

—June Havoc, award-winning singer and stage director

"I don't need easy, I just need possible."

—Bethany Hamilton, shark attack survivor and award-winning competitive surfer

Bethany Hamilton

In 1998, at the age of eight, Hawaii native Bethany Hamilton began surfing at a competitive level, receiving her first sponsorship a year later at the age of nine. By the year she turned thirteen, she finished second in the open women's division of the National Scholastic Surfing Association's National Championships.

Her life was forever changed on the morning of October 31, 2003, when she went surfing with her best friend, Alana, and Alana's father and brother. During the surf expedition, she was attacked by a fourteen-foot tiger shark. The shark completely severed her left arm, causing her to lose over 60 percent of her blood and to go into hypovolemic shock. Alana's father, after fashioning a makeshift tourniquet from his surfboard leash, rushed her to the closest hospital.

She spent over three months in the hospital recovering before she was allowed to go home. Yet despite the extremely traumatic shark attack and now only having one arm, Hamilton was determined to return to surfing as soon as she possibly could. She had to start using a new board with a handle for her right arm and relearn how to surf. Many were shocked by her perseverance in continuing to surf and compete, but that determination did not go unacknowledged. Hamilton earned the ESPY Award for Best Comeback Athlete, the Courage Teen Choice Award, and many others. She has been featured on many TV shows, including *The Oprah Winfrey Show* and *The Ellen DeGeneres Show*. She went on to publish several books, including *Devotions for the Soul Surfer* and *Body and Soul: A Girl's Guide to a Fit, Fun and Fabulous Life*. Her incredible story inspired the creation of the film *Soul Surfer*.

Hamilton went on to compete on *The Amazing Race*, finishing third, and took first place at the Surf 'n' Sea Pipeline Women's Pro in 2014. She produced a documentary about her life, *Unstoppable*, which premiered in 2018.

Hamilton is now married with three children, living in the beautiful paradise of Kauai and continuing to surf competitively. She is a force of nature—a woman who has proved to be truly unstoppable.

Affirmation Station

I will treat my body better starting today.
I know what I need to be my best self.
I have everything inside of me I need to care for myself.

"Live as if you like yourself, and it may happen."

—Marge Piercy, progressive writer, poet, and activist whose work covers feminism and political activism

"Don't compromise yourself. You are all you've got."

—Janis Joplin, remarkable singer-songwriter whose tunes ranged from rock and roll and soul to the blues

"A strong woman looks a challenge in the eye and gives it a wink."

—Gina Carey, independent filmmaker and soul/R & B/gospel music singer

"A really strong woman accepts the war she went through and is ennobled by her scars."

–Carly Simon, singer and songwriter who had multiple hit songs and was inducted into the Rock & Roll Hall of Fame in 2022

"We can't see the beauty in everything that we are because we've been taught to first see everything that we're not."

–Megan Jayne Crabbe, body positivity activist, social media influencer, eating disorder survivor, and author of *Body Positive Power*

Laverne Cox

Growing up in Alabama in the 1970s, Cox always felt she was a woman although she was born biologically male. Her ways of expressing her femininity were met with ruthless teasing and scrutiny by her peers. She found an outlet with dance when her mother enrolled her in jazz and tap in the third grade. Cox went on to study at the Alabama School of Fine Arts before attending college, where she graduated with a Bachelor of Fine Arts in Dance. It was in college that she began the process of medically transitioning from male to female.

Her love of the arts continued as she pursued acting, finding success on both primetime and reality television programs. She finally landed her breakout role as Sophia Burset on the Netflix series *Orange Is the New Black*. The character of Sophia was also a trans woman, one who fought for appropriate hormone treatments within the women's prison system. Cox has also appeared on other television programs as trans characters, showcasing the legendary role of Frank N. Furter in the 2016 remake of the classic musical *The Rocky Horror Picture Show*.

Cox is the first openly transgender person in history to receive an Emmy nomination for her powerful performance as Sophie, as well as the first to appear on the cover of *TIME* magazine. She writes her own column for *The Huffington Post* as a trans rights advocate, and she executive produced the documentaries *The T Word*, which follows the lives of trans youth, and *Free CeCe*, which tells the story of an imprisoned trans woman. She won an Emmy for her role as executive producer of *The T Word*, the first trans woman to do so. Cox appeared on the February 2018 cover of *Cosmopolitan*, the first openly transgender cover girl in the magazine's history.

Laverne Cox remains a true warrior of the transgender community as she continues to portray strong trans characters onscreen and fight for trans rights offscreen.

"At the end of the day, we can endure much more than we think we can."

–Frida Kahlo, renowned painter known for her many portraits, self-portraits, and works inspired by the nature and artifacts of Mexico

"I am not like everyone else. I don't pretend to be. I don't want to be. I am me."

–Grace VanderWaal, singer-songwriter and actress known for her distinctive vocals and ukulele playing

Embrace Your Inner Goddess

Beauty comes from the inside; so if you are a self-accepting, kind, and loving person, you will radiate that inner beauty to the outside, and that is what people will see just as much as anything else. This is what matters!

Loving one's body opens us up to a world of possibilities. When we love ourselves in the physical world, it allows our hearts and minds to grow in beautiful ways as well. Confidence makes us brave. It makes us fearless. When we love ourselves, we don't let anyone push us around or take advantage of our vulnerability. We become fierce warriors who are virtually bulletproof.

This is not always easy. It is very simple to say that you love yourself just as you are, but it is another to live it daily. There are days when everyone—even the supposedly perfect model—finds a flaw in herself that she cannot ignore. And that's okay because we are all human. Guess what? Human bodies are flawed. But these "flaws" just add something special to the whole beautiful picture.

A woman's body has the power to do many bold and empowering things. I want you to know that you can do such things: Just as you are, right now, you can speak boldly, protest loudly, and love and live freely in the body that you possess right now.

Allow yourself to do that.

Your body is beautiful. It's important to tell yourself that every day.

Chapter 3

THE POWER OF POSITIVITY

Find Your Happy Place

"Just stay positive!" This is something all of us are told countless times during the course of our lives. It is easier said than done—but it is something that is essential to maintaining a healthy lifestyle and supporting well-being. It is very easy to get caught up in the difficulties we face on a daily basis. And while we need to face these in whatever way we are able, living a life of positivity is one of the best ways.

It may be as simple as flipping the script: Don't think of it as, "I have to remain positive today." Think of it as finding ways of spreading joy and happiness to those around you. Positivity is a powerful thing that can make a huge difference to you and those you love. Look at your life and find ways you can spin things in a better direction: Are you giving to others, or are you a little out of balance, where your work and your immediate family get 99 percent of what you offer the world? You can change that in one day. Donate more of your time or money to a charity. Supporting a cause will help keep you informed about social issues and can strengthen your sense of well-being while benefiting others in the process.

Bringing joy to others is one of the best and most beautiful ways of bringing more positivity into your life. Being a source of happiness in another person's day can be extremely rewarding. To put this into practice, try thinking of how someone has turned a bad day of yours into a joyful one. Did you receive a text from a friend or family member that instantly made you feel better? Was there someone who helped you with a task at work that you were finding overwhelming? Take these small (but nonetheless important) things and find ways to give that positivity back. There are many ways you can plant the seed of happiness today—whether it be wishing someone a great day, complimenting someone's talents, or helping someone without being asked. You never know how much another person may need it. Scatter the seed of happiness wherever you go and watch it grow!

Affirmation Station

I will count my blessings.
I choose to focus on the good things.
I vow to give back when I can.

Make Your Kindness Contagious

"The little things" are not so little—especially not to some. Minimal action items such as holding the door for someone or letting someone go ahead of you in line can mean the world to them. We live in a world of connected chaos: We are always reachable and always on the go. In the midst of all of this rushing around, we can forget the feelings of those around us. A simple gesture is just that: simple, yet it can be quite impactful and make a difference to you as well as to others.

In the beautiful paradise known as the Hawaiian Islands, there is a tradition of "Living Aloha."

This phrase can mean love, affection, compassion, mercy, sympathy, pity, kindness, or grace. It is the coordination of mind and heart within each person—it brings each person to the core of their inner self. Each person must think and express good feelings to others.

Spreading positivity to those around you as well as reminding yourself about all you have to be grateful for is a practice that costs nothing yet has incredible value. It allows you to feed your soul as well as others who may need it.

Take Note of the Good

Start to notice and write down all the positive things in your life that make your day a little brighter. Do this for a week and evaluate how it made you feel.

Affirmation Station

I will do something for someone else today.
I am going to be positive no matter what the day holds.
I want to bring happiness to others.

Take the Harder Road to Happiness

It isn't always easy to be positive, especially when life takes a painful turn. Experiencing unexpected change can make it easy to turn to anger or frustration. Pushing past those immediate feelings to reach a better place can feel impossible. But it's not. And we all have those days, and it can feel as if they will consume us. But once you find yourself coming back to a better, brighter place (and we all do this at our own pace), the end result of capturing one's lost joy cannot be beat.

Positivity has an uncanny ability to affect us both physically and mentally. Keeping a positive attitude keeps our heart healthy, our blood pressure down, and our immune systems strong. But more than that, it keeps our minds sharp and open to possibility. When we look on the bright side no matter what hand we've been dealt, we put forth beautiful energy into the universe—it may come back when we need it, or go to someone else who needs it now. Nonetheless, while happiness is the harder endeavor, it is always the most worthwhile.

> *"Keep your face to the sunshine and you cannot see a shadow."*
>
> —Helen Keller, author, disability rights advocate, political activist, and lecturer who lost her sight and hearing after a bout of illness at the age of nineteen months

> *"Try to be a rainbow in someone's cloud."*
>
> —Maya Angelou, prolific poet, memoirist, singer, and civil rights activist

> *"With the new day comes new strength and new thoughts."*
>
> —Eleanor Roosevelt, political figure, diplomat, and activist who was the wife of Franklin D. Roosevelt, the thirty-second President of the United States

Affirmation Station

I will be kind to myself.
My needs matter.
I deserve good things.

"I just think happiness is what makes you pretty. Period. Happy people are beautiful."

—Drew Barrymore, actress who overcame addiction and childhood trauma and went on to have a successful film and television career both in front of and behind the camera

"It's your outlook on life that counts. If you take yourself lightly and don't take yourself too seriously, pretty soon you can find the humor in our everyday lives. And sometimes it can be a lifesaver."

—Betty White, pioneer actress of television and film who broke down barriers for women in the entertainment industry and went on to have a career of over seventy years in front of the camera

"Hope is the most exciting thing there is in life."

—Mandy Moore, singer, songwriter, and actress known for her work on television and film

"Adopting a really positive attitude can work wonders to adding years to your life, a spring to your step, a sparkle to your eye, and all of that."

—Christie Brinkley, model, actress and entrepreneur who has appeared on over 500 magazine covers

"Words can break someone into a million pieces, but they can also put them back together. I hope you use yours for good."

—Taylor Swift, genre-crossing singer-songwriter known for her deeply personal song lyrics

---

Affirmation Station

I am a can-do person.

I am worthy.

I am here.

"You grow up the day you have your first real laugh at yourself."

—Ethel Barrymore, stage, screen, and radio actress whose career spanned six decades

Mary Oliver

In 2007, the *New York Times* described Mary Oliver as the country's bestselling poet. Her work has won numerous awards, including the Pulitzer Prize, the National Book Award, and a Lannan Literary Award for Lifetime Achievement. In commentary on *Dream Work* (1986) in *The Nation*, reviewer Alicia Ostriker described Oliver as one of America's finest poets, writing that Oliver was as "visionary as Emerson."

Born in 1935, Oliver was raised in Maple Hills Heights, outside Cleveland, Ohio, where her father was a history teacher and athletics coach in the public schools. As a child, she used the nearby woods as a retreat from a difficult home, having experienced abuse at an early age; there she would write poems. Though she attended both Ohio State University and Vassar College, she did not receive a degree from either institution. As a young poet, Oliver was deeply influenced by Edna St. Vincent Millay; she even lived in Millay's home, "Steepletop," and helped Norma Millay organize her sister's papers for half a dozen years. After meeting her eventual life partner, Molly Malone Cook, the couple moved to Provincetown, Massachusetts; in *Our World*, a book of Cook's photos and journal entries Oliver compiled after Cook's death, she describes their meeting: "I took one look [at Molly] and fell, hook and tumble." Cook became Oliver's literary agent. The

surrounding Cape Cod landscape of their new home found
its way into Oliver's work. Known for its clarity and expressive
reliance on imagery involving the natural world, Oliver's poetry
is grounded in a sense of place and in the nature tradition of the
Romantic movement.

Mary Oliver's first collection of poetry, 1963's *No Voyage and
Other Poems*, was published when she was twenty-eight. (She
taught at Case Western University in the early '80s.) Critics took
notice of her early on, and 1983's *American Primitive*, her fifth
book, won a Pulitzer Prize. *Dream Work* (1986) continued her
quest to "understand both the wonder and pain of nature,"
according to *LA Times* book reviewer Holly Prado. Striker of *The
Nation* declared Oliver "among the few American poets who
can describe and transmit ecstasy while retaining a practical
awareness of the world as one of predators and prey." She
started to transition to more personal realms in 1992's *New and
Selected Poems*, which won the National Book Award. Writing
in the *LA Times Book Review*, critic Susan Salter Reynolds
noted that Oliver's early poems were nearly always oriented
toward nature and seldom examined the self. In contrast,
Oliver presents her own voice constantly in her later works.
Nonetheless, Oliver continued to celebrate the natural world in
her works *Winter Hours: Prose, Prose Poems, and Poems* (1999),
Why I Wake Early (2004), *New and Selected Poems, Volume
2* (2004), and *Swan: Poems and Prose Poems* (2010). Oliver

has been compared by literary critics to other great American lyric poets and celebrators of nature such as Marianne Moore, Elizabeth Bishop, Edna St. Vincent Millay, and Walt Whitman.

A prolific writer, Oliver published a new book every year or two. Her main themes continued to be the intersection between the human and the natural world. The books she wrote late in life include *A Thousand Mornings* (2012), *Dog Songs* (2013), *Blue Horses* (2014), *Felicity* (2015), *Upstream: Selected Essays* (2016), and *Devotions: The Selected Poems of Mary Oliver* (2017). She held a chair at Bennington College until 2001. Besides the Pulitzer Prize and National Book Award, Oliver also received fellowships from the Guggenheim Foundation and the National Endowment for the Arts; she was a winner of the American Academy of Arts & Letters Award, the Poetry Society of America's Shelley Memorial Prize, and the Alice Fay di Castagnola Award.

Mary Oliver lived in Provincetown, Massachusetts, and Hobe Sound, Florida, until her passing at age eighty-three in early 2019.

> *"The best way to show my gratitude is to accept everything, even my problems, with joy."*
> —Mother Teresa, nun and missionary who has been honored as a saint within the Catholic Church and is known for her incredible humanitarian work

---

Affirmation Station

I choose me.
I am confident and strong!
My inner beauty shines brightly.

"Dance from your heart and love your music, and the audience will love you in return."

—Maria Tallchief, indigenous dancer who was both the first major prima ballerina in America was well as the first Native American woman to ever hold a prima ballerina title

"I have spent a lifetime trying to share what it has meant to be a woman first in the world of sports so that other young women will have a chance to reach their dreams."

—Wilma Rudolph, sprinter, record-holding Olympic champion, and international sports icon in track and field

Wilma Rudolph

Runner Wilma Rudolph's life is the story of a great spirit and heart overcoming obstacles that would have stopped anyone else in their tracks, literally! Born in Bethlehem, Tennessee, in

1955, Rudolph contracted polio at the age of four and was left with a useless leg.

Rudolph's family was in dire straits with a total of eighteen children from her father's two marriages. Both parents worked constantly to feed the burgeoning brood, her father as a porter and her mother as a house cleaner; and it was more important to feed Rudolph and her siblings than it was to get the medical attention she needed to recover the use of her leg. Two years later, circumstances eased a bit, and at the age of six, Rudolph started riding the back of the bus with her mother to Nashville twice a week for physical therapy. Although doctors predicted she would never walk without braces, Rudolph kept up her rehabilitation program for five years, and not only did the braces come off, but "by the time I was twelve," as she told the *Chicago Tribune*, "I was challenging every boy in the neighborhood at running, jumping, everything."

Her exceptional ability didn't go unnoticed. A coach with Tennessee State University saw how she was winning every race she entered in high school and offered to train her for the Olympics, which Rudolph hadn't even heard of. Nevertheless, she qualified for the Olympics at sixteen and took home a bronze medal in the 1956 Summer Games for the 100-meter relay. Still in high school, she decided to work toward winning a gold medal at the 1960 Games.

Well, she did that and more. The three gold medals she won in the 1960 Olympics in Rome—in the 100-meter dash, the 200-meter dash, and the 4 x 100 relay—turned her into a superstar overnight. Rudolph was the first American woman ever to win triple gold in a single Olympics. People were stumbling over the top of each other to find the superlatives to describe her. The French named her "La Gazelle," and in America she was known as "The Fastest Woman on Earth." Rudolph was everybody's darling after that, with invitations to the JFK White House and numerous guest appearances on television. The flip side of all the glory, however, was that Rudolph received hardly any financial reward for her public appearances and had to work odd jobs to get through college.

One year later, Rudolph again set the world on fire by breaking the record for the 100-meter dash: 11.2 seconds.

Unpredictably, she sat out the '64 Olympic Games and stayed in school, graduating with a degree in education and returning to the very school she had attended as a youngster to teach second grade. In 1967, she worked for the Job Corps and Operation Champion, a program that endeavored to bring star athletes into American ghettos as positive role models for young kids. Rudolph herself loved to talk to kids about sports and was a powerful symbol with her inspiring story.

That Wilma Rudolph touched the lives of children is best evidenced in a letter writing campaign taken up by a class of fourth graders in Jessup, Maryland, who requested the World Book Encyclopedia correct their error in excluding the world-class athlete. The publisher complied immediately! Rudolph has also been honored with induction into both the Olympic Hall of Fame and the National Track and Field Hall of Fame. A film version of her autobiography *Wilma* starring Cicely Tyson was produced to tremendous acclaim. Her death at only fifty-four from brain cancer took place shortly after she received an honor as one of "The Great Ones" at the premiere National Sports Awards in 1993.

> *"When you have a dream, you've got to grab it and never let go."*
>
> —Carol Burnett, legendary actress and comedian known for her groundbreaking variety series *The Carol Burnett Show*

> *"Inspiration comes when you let go."*
>
> —Yuan Yuan Tan, prima ballerina at the San Francisco Ballet who has been called the greatest Chinese ballerina of all time

Affirmation Station

I approve of me.

I accept myself.

I love me.

"My recipe for life is not being afraid of myself, afraid of what I think, or of my opinions."

—Eartha Kitt, singer, actress, dancer, and comedian famous for her distinctive singing style

Affirmation Station

I am enough.

I can love me.

My words have value.

"If you can't change your fate, change your attitude."

—Amy Tan, bestselling author who wrote the famous novel *The Joy Luck Club*

"The goal isn't to live forever, but to create something that will."

—Selena, Mexican American singer known as the "Queen of Tejano music"

Affirmation Station

I am overcoming my insecurities.

I provide immense self-fulfillment.

Feeling confident is a natural part of my life.

"Know what sparks the light in you so that you, in your own way, can illuminate the world."

—Oprah Winfrey, television producer, actress, talk-show host, author, and philanthropist who is often ranked as the most influential woman in the world

"One of the first steps to happiness is deciding that you want to be happy and knowing what that means. I have had many full-on conversations about what that looks like for me. To be happy is a choice you make every day, every hour. And refining and renewing that state is a constant pursuit."

—Julia Roberts, actress known for her leading roles in multiple films over the last three decades who has won both an Academy Award and several Golden Globes

"I'm gonna take this world by storm. Pun intended."

—Storm Reid, child actress who currently stars in the groundbreaking HBO drama *Euphoria*

Edith Wharton

I wonder what Edith Wharton, Henry James, and Jane Austen would think if they realized that long after the span of their own lifetimes, their works rule Hollywood as favorite novels-turned-movies? Henry James, mentor to Edith Wharton, would probably not be surprised at their dominion over the current fascination with social mores. James couldn't seem to reach high enough heights with his hyperbolic praise for Wharton, calling her "the whirling princess, the great and glorious pendulum, the gyrator, the devil-dancer, the golden eagle, the Fire Bird, the Shining One, the angel of desolation or of devastation, the historic ravager."

Born in 1862 in New York to a wealthy family, Edith Newbold
Jones was from the privileged background she described in
her novels. She summered in Newport, Rhode Island, and lived
abroad in Italy, Germany, and France, riding out the depression
that immediately followed the Civil War and affected her
family's fortunes.

She was homeschooled by a governess and prepared for her
debut into society at the age of seventeen. Unlike many of her
fellow debs, however, she was already writing. The teenager
took her craft very seriously, and at sweet sixteen, produced
a volume of poetry that her parents had printed despite their
misgivings about her pursuit of writing as a career. She also
read insatiably, devouring the books in her father's library;
otherwise, she claimed, her "mind would have starved at the
age when the mental muscles are most in need of feeding....
I was enthralled by words.... Wherever I went they sang to me
like the birds in an enchanted forest."

In 1885, she married Edward "Teddy" Robbins Wharton, the
son of an elite Boston family. Teddy was thirteen years her
senior, and they quickly created a life reflecting their genteel
parentage. Sadly, her husband was not her intellectual match
and had few interests in that direction; he was more interested
in having children, which rapidly became a major issue in their
marriage. They remained childless and kept up a facade of

compatibility to the world. Meanwhile, she struggled to write on a level in accordance with her own ambitions, finally getting her inspiration and footing after a voyage through the Greek Isles. She then wrote and published a series of very well-received articles for *Scribner's*, *Harper's*, and *Century* magazines, and even went on to collaborate with a Boston architect, Ogden Codman, Jr., on a book entitled *The Decoration of Houses* in 1897.

Despite these efforts, she fell into a severe depression she called her "paralyzing melancholy" and had to get a "rest cure" for nervous illnesses. In 1899, two collections of her short stories were published, coinciding with the end of her nervous condition and depression. After this, she consigned herself to writing completely and published a book a year for the remainder of her life. In 1905, with *The House of Mirth*, she achieved the height of her power and range as a writer. Subsequent novels, such as *The Reef*, *The Custom of the Country*, and *The Age of Innocence*, caused comparisons to her friend and counselor, describing her as a "female Henry James." She was clearly on her own track, while also making a study of symbolists such as Joseph Conrad and the modern musical compositions of Igor Stravinsky.

Wharton began an affair with a member of her literary circle, James's protégé Morton Fullerton. While the Whartons' marriage crumbled around them, she and Teddy sold their stately Lenox home, "The Mount," and moved to France. Teddy suffered a nervous breakdown and checked into a Swiss sanatorium; he divorced her in 1913. She remained in Europe, making a home for herself in France.

Wharton found the life of a divorcee to be revelatory. She could travel, entertain, write, and have friendships with men without any interference. She also got involved in public and political affairs, and among her significant charity works, founded shelters for refugees during World War I.

In 1930, Wharton was elected to the National Institute of Arts and Letters, and four years later, to the American Academy of Arts and Letters. She lived to the age of seventy-five, at which time she had a fatal stroke. During her life of letters, she contributed enormously to the novel form. Her subtlety and sophistication continue to bring her books to many readers far beyond the bounds of the new elites of Hollywood.

> *"I've come to believe that seeking happiness is not a frivolous pursuit. It's honorable and necessary. And most people forget to even think about it."*
>
> —Goldie Hawn, actress, producer, and singer whose career has spanned decades

"Just to be alive is a grand thing."

—Agatha Christie, author of more than sixty books, who currently stands as the bestselling novelist of all time

---

Affirmation Station

I am internally confident.

I exude inner strength.

I am extremely powerful.

"Optimism is the fuel driving every fight I've been in."

—Vice President Kamala Harris, attorney and politician who is the first woman and first American of color to hold this position

"The power of finding beauty in the humblest things makes home happy and life lovely."

—Louisa May Alcott, author of the beloved classic *Little Women* and its sequels

"I discovered that joy is not the negation of pain, but rather acknowledging the presence of pain and feeling happiness in spite of it."

—Lupita Nyong'o, actress known for her groundbreaking work in the films *Black Panther*, *Us*, and *12 Years A Slave*, the last of which earned her an Academy Award

"When life puts you in a tough situation, don't say, 'Why me,' say, 'Try me.' "

—Miley Cyrus, actress and singer who is known for her versatile vocals

---

Affirmation Station

I will see things in a positive light.
I am capable of seeing the silver lining.
I know I am blessed.

"Love yourself first and everything else falls into line. You really have to love yourself to get anything done in this world."

—Lucille Ball, actress whose groundbreaking show *I Love Lucy* was one of the first family-based sitcoms covering a wide range of topics, including pregnancy, marital issues, women in the workplace, and suburban living, all of which were somewhat controversial at the time

"This is what we know for sure: At some point in our lives, we will all be broken and bruised—but we are not alone. We find joy together. We persevere together."

—Dr. Jill Biden, educator and political figure who is currently the First Lady of the United States

"Being optimistic is like a muscle that gets stronger with use."

—Robin Roberts, television broadcaster, anchor, and the first woman of color and first member of the LGBTQIA+ community to host *Jeopardy!*

"If you're happy, then you win, and then you win because you're happy."

—Serena Williams, professional tennis player who has won twenty-three Grand Slam titles, the most of any player in the Open Era

Find Your Own Rainbow

It may feel like an impossibility to be positive right now. But wherever you are or whatever cards life has handed you, seeing the big picture in a bright, beautiful light will have so many benefits in the long run. While we should be able to take time to feel whatever it is we need to feel, it should always circle back to a place of positivity. Self-dedication to staying optimistic is not just for ourselves—it's also for those around us who need the same boost of serotonin. While we should always work to be positive within our own lives, supporting others in this journey is just as important.

Make it a habit to take notice of everything around you: the sun in the sky, the birds in the trees, the soft breeze on your face—anything that brings a smile to your face. Paint your toenails pink! Bake your famous chocolate chip cookies! Pour a cup of coffee and read a beloved book! Doing the things that bring you joy and happiness will reap a harvest of positivity. And the best news? When we have too much, we can share it with others, which is often the best part of all.

Chapter 4

SAYING NO / SETTING BOUNDARIES LIKE A BOSS

No As A Mantra

No—this is a word we often heard as children whenever we wanted something, whether it was a new toy or an extra cookie. And in correlation with that, many of us, myself included, were raised to accommodate others. Even if you didn't want to do something, you were told to obey in order to be polite. Women in particular all throughout history have been told that "no" is not an option: Women were forced into marriages with men they didn't know or love and told that their opinions and ideas did not matter, and the list goes on.

Now, as we experience adulthood as badass women, I have a message for all of us: You Do Not Have To Do Anything You Don't Want To Do. Say it. Sing it. Shout it from the rooftops.

The No Principle can be applied to any part of our lives we want. If you do not want to attend an event, you are allowed to say no and stay home to rest and give yourself some much-needed self-care. If you are overwhelmed at work and do not have the bandwidth to take on extra projects, you are within your rights to say no. If anyone is trying to convince you that you should live your life a certain way—you should hurry up and get married, have kids before it's too late, etc.—if these are things you do not want or need, say no. Find the satisfaction is knowing what is best for you as a human, and do not feel any guilt for being honest with yourself or others.

Affirmation Station

I am always allowed to say no.
I will not let anyone tell me what to do.
I am a person in control of my own destiny.

You Don't Own Me

Setting boundaries for ourselves is a vital part of establishing independence as a badass individual. It is not only healthy, but also essential. These lines should be drawn in the workplace as well as in our personal lives. At work, it is very easy to convince ourselves we must be a team player and volunteer our time in any way that we can. While this is something we can often do, that is not always the case. We must stand up for ourselves and not allow others to walk all over us.

It is just as important, if not more so, to set these boundaries within our personal lives. Finding our own levels of comfort when it comes to physical space and emotional vulnerability is a key part of knowing where our own boundaries are. If there is a person in your life who does not respect your physical or emotional space, draw a line in the sand and maintain distance. This is not something to feel any guilt about—feeling safe as a human is crucial and is not to be taken lightly.

Affirmation Station

I will let my guard down when I am comfortable.
I am a strong woman who will not be manipulated.
I will not allow anyone to make me feel inferior.

Communication Is Key

When it comes to relationships, boundaries have many layers. These boundaries can be physical as well as emotional. Friendships can test boundaries just as easily as romantic entanglements can. Friends can step over the line and hurt us in a number of ways. It is important that we are clear in our communication when someone oversteps. While this is not always easy, we should not let a close friend or family member create chaos within our lives. Holding such boundaries can be an incredibly difficult thing to do that is much easier said than done, but it is often necessary to embrace that discomfort in order to take a stand.

Maintaining boundaries and saying no in general is very easy for some (I salute you!). If that is the case for you and if you see a fellow badass woman struggling with this, support them. Let them know your magical secrets of setting those important boundaries and standing your ground. There is strength in numbers.

Pat Yourself on the Back

As children in our society, we're taught to give most of our attention to things about ourselves that are in need of correction rather than what's great about us; this is emphasized doubly in the socialization of girls and women. We are conditioned to criticize ourselves. But what we're doing *right* is at least as important as our flaws and imperfections.

Take note of your own "superpowers," and make it a goal to take notice of when you accomplish something and acknowledge yourself for having done it.

"My goal now is to remember every place that I've been, only do the things I love, and not say yes when I don't mean it."

—Sandra Bullock, actress, producer, and recipient of multiple awards who was the highest-paid actress in 2010 and 2014

"There are reasons to set boundaries for yourself, but there are also reasons to keep doors open."

—Ashley Graham, television presenter and supermodel who is an advocate for the body positivity movement

"I swear to God, the second I learned how to say 'no,' I felt that was the best anti-aging I could do for myself."

—Gabrielle Union, actress who has appeared on television and film, famous for her roles in *Bring It On* and *Being Mary Jane*

Affirmation Station

I am the keeper of my own journey.
I decide when I want to pursue something.
My goals are my own.

"I think that a big part of being a feminist is to make sure that young women know that they have rights and that they have bodily autonomy; that they can say no."

—Sophia Pierre-Antoine, feminist who has worked for the past few years on women and girls' rights

"No is a complete sentence."

—Anne Lamott, novelist and political activist known for covering controversial topics such as religion, mental health, and substance abuse

Affirmation Station

I am in charge.
I decide what I do.
I am the driver of my own life.

*"Women will have achieved true equality when men
share with them the responsibility of bringing up the
next generation."*

—Ruth Bader Ginsberg, lawyer who served as an associate
justice of the Supreme Court of the United States for twenty-
seven years

Ruth Bader Ginsberg

Born in 1933 as Ruth Joan Bader, she grew up in a Jewish family
in a working-class neighborhood in Brooklyn, New York. Her
mother supported the family by working in a garment factory
and actively encouraged her to pursue her education. (Sadly,
her mother died the day before Ruth's high school graduation.)
She graduated first in her class from Cornell University in
1954, then married fellow law student Martin Ginsberg after
graduating; they had their first child in 1955.

She went on to continue her law education at Harvard
University, where she was one of five female students in a class
of 500. She pushed past these barriers and became a member
of the Harvard Law Review. She transferred to Columbia Law
School in New York City, where she graduated yet again first
in her class in 1959. Despite her academic achievements, she
was passed over for several law positions due to her gender.
She worked as a clerk before she began teaching law at both

Rutgers University and Columbia University, becoming the
latter institution's first female professor. She served as the
director of the Women's Rights Project of the American Civil
Liberties Union, on whose behalf she argued several gender
discrimination cases before the US Supreme Court, one of
which actually involved the rights of men (as she believed
everyone was entitled to equal rights) in the case of Social
Security Act provisions that granted benefits to widows but
not widowers.

In 1980, President Jimmy Carter appointed Ginsberg to the US
Court of Appeals, where she served until she was appointed
to the US Supreme Court in 1998 by President Bill Clinton
and confirmed by the Senate in a 96-3 vote. She became the
second female justice as well as the first Jewish female justice
to serve on the court. She was the author of the decision behind
United States v. Virginia, which stated that the Virginia Military
Institute could not refuse to admit women. She was awarded the
Thurgood Marshall Award in 1999 for her contributions to civil
rights and gender equality.

After serving as a Supreme Court justice for twenty-seven years,
she passed away in 2020 due to metastatic pancreatic cancer
at the age of eighty-seven. Ruth Bader Ginsberg will always be
remembered as someone who did not hesitate to fight back
when she saw any group being discriminated against. Her

dedication to the rights of women and workers proves that she truly was a voice for us all.

> *"I always wanted to be a femme fatale. Even when I was a young girl, I never really wanted to be a girl. I wanted to be a woman."*

–Diane Von Furstenberg, fashion designer who started a clothing line now available in over seventy counties

---

Affirmation Station

I am not afraid.

I am brave.

I will not let anyone take that from me.

> *"I encourage women to step up. Don't wait for somebody to ask you."*

–Reese Witherspoon, actress and producer who has won multiple awards and starred in over fifty films

> *"Above all, be the heroine of your life, not the victim."*

–Nora Ephron, filmmaker, journalist, and author who directed multiple award-winning films

"If you don't see a clear path for what you want, sometimes you have to make it yourself."

—Mindy Kaling, actress, comedian, and screenwriter widely known for her performance as Kelly on the award-winning series *The Office*

"I am learning every day to allow the space between where I am and where I want to be to inspire me and not terrify me."

—Tracee Ellis Ross, actress, singer, producer, and businesswoman known for her television roles in *Girlfriends* and *Black-ish*

Katherine Johnson

Katherine Johnson was an African American woman who made mathematical and research contributions to the early development of US space flight despite racial and gender discrimination.

Born in 1918 in White Sulphur Springs, West Virginia, she developed a curiosity for numbers and proved to have a brilliant mind at a young age; she skipped several grades. She enrolled in West Virginia State College at eighteen, going on to graduate with the highest honors in 1937 and take a teaching position at a local public school.

After getting married and attending a graduate math program, Johnson began working at the National Advisory Committee for Aeronautics (NACA) Langley laboratory in Hampton, Virginia, in 1953. Soon after, she was assigned to the Maneuver Loads Branch of the Flight Research Division.

In 1957, when the Soviets launched Sputnik, it changed the course of history and Johnson's life as well. She would go on to provide the math for the 1958 document Notes on Space Technology, a series of lectures given by engineers in the Flight Research Division and the Pilotless Aircraft Research Division. Engineers from these groups formed the Space Task Group, the NACA's first foray into space travel.

Johnson would go on to do analysis for the first human spaceflight and coauthor a report on methods for laying out equations describing an orbital spaceflight (equations by which the landing position was specified), making her the first woman in the division to receive credit on a research report.

In 1962, as NASA prepared for John Glenn's mission, Johnson was called upon to run the necessary numbers for the equations by hand on her desktop mechanical calculating machine. Although these had been programmed into the computer, Glenn said to "get the girl" to check them. "If she says they're good, then I'm ready to go," he said. His flight was a success, marking a turning point for the US in space.

By her retirement, she had worked on the space shuttle and authored or coauthored twenty-six research reports. At the age of ninety-seven, she was awarded the Presidential Medal of Freedom by President Barack Obama. She lived to be 101, passing away peacefully on February 24, 2020. Katherine Johnson will always be remembered as a trailblazer and pioneer for women in science.

> *"Vulnerability sounds like truth and feels like courage. Truth and courage aren't always comfortable, but they're never weakness."*
>
> —Brené Brown, professor, lecturer, author, and podcast host known in particular for her research on leadership, vulnerability, and courage

> *"There's something special about a woman who dominates in a man's world. It takes a certain grace, strength, intelligence, fearlessness, and the nerve to never take no for an answer."*
>
> —Rihanna, singer, actress, and fashion designer who has sold over 250 million records

Affirmation Station

I am leading my own life.

I can turn down an invitation.

I do not owe anyone anything.

"I never had confidence—never. The hardest thing to know is your own worth, and it took me years and years to find out what mine is."

—Peggy Lipton, actress, model, and singer famous for her role as Julie Barnes in *The Mod Squad* series

"Becoming acquainted with yourself is a price well worth paying for the love that will really address your needs."

—Daphne Rose Kingma, therapist, relationship expert, and author of a dozen books about love, relationships, and living through crisis

"Fearlessness is like a muscle. I know from my own life that the more I exercise it, the more natural it becomes to not let my fears run me."

—Arianna Huffington, author, columnist, and businesswoman who is the cofounder of *The Huffington Post*

Affirmation Station

I will set my own boundaries.
I will say no when I choose to.
I do not owe anyone my time.

"*This life is mine alone. So I have stopped asking people for directions to places they've never been.*"

—Glennon Doyle, author and activist known for her novels that shook up the internet

"*Being authentic and honest with everyone is the best way to figure out who you are.*"

—Demi Lovato, singer, songwriter, and actor who has been open about their recovery from addiction and self-harm

"*Yes, the more successful you are—or the stronger, the more opinionated—the less you will be generally liked. All of a sudden people will think you're too 'braggy,' too loud, too something. But the tradeoff is undoubtedly worth it. Power and authenticity are worth it.*"

—Jessica Valenti, feminist writer who has authored multiple books and is the cofounder of the blog *Feministing*

"Celebrate who you are. Say, 'This is my kingdom.' "

–Salma Hayek, actress who portrayed Frida Kahlo
in the biographical film *Frida*, earning an Academy
Award nomination

Affirmation Station

I know myself better than anyone.
I will refuse to do something if I choose.
I am powerful and I can be unmoving.

---

*"No society can or will prosper without the cooperation
of women."*

–Lee Tai-young, attorney who was Korea's first female lawyer

Lee Tai-young

Lee Tai-young was the first Korean woman ever to become a
lawyer and a judge as well as the founder of the first Korean
legal aid center. She was born in what is now North Korea in
1914, the daughter of a gold miner. She received a degree in
home economics from Ewha Womans University, a Methodist

college, and married a Methodist minister in 1936. Tai-young
had dreams of becoming a lawyer when she came to Seoul
to study at Ewha, but when her husband fell under suspicion
of being a spy for the US and was jailed for sedition by the
Japanese colonial government in the early 1940s, she had to go
to work to maintain her family. She took jobs as a schoolteacher
and a radio singer, as well as taking in sewing and washing.

After the war, Tai-young continued her studies with the support
of her husband. In 1946, she became the first woman to attend
Seoul National University and went on to earn her law degree in
1949. She was the first woman ever to pass the National Judicial
Examination in 1952. Five years later, she founded the Women's
Legal Counseling Center, a law practice that provided services
to poor women. She and her husband were participants in the
1976 Myeongdong Declaration, which called for the return of
civil liberties to Korean citizens. Because of her political views,
she was arrested as an enemy of President Park Chung-hee,
and in 1977, she received a three-year suspended sentence
along with a loss of civil liberties, including being automatically
disbarred for ten years.

Her law practice evolved into the Korea Legal Aid Center for
Family Relations, a substantial office serving more than 10,000
clients per year. She authored fifteen books on women's issues,
beginning with a 1957 guide to Korea's divorce system. In 1972,

she published *Commonsense in Law for Women*; other notable titles include *Born A Woman* and *The Woman of North Korea*. She also translated Eleanor Roosevelt's book *On My Own* into Korean. In 1975, the Ramon Magsaysay Award Foundation chose her as the recipient of their Community Leadership Award; she was given an award by the International Legal Aid Association in 1978. She received international recognition from many quarters, including an honorary law doctorate from Drew University in Madison, NJ in 1981. In 1984, she published a memoir, *Dipping the Han River Out with a Gourd*, four years before she passed away at the ripe old age of eighty-four.

> *"I am not free while any woman is unfree, even when her shackles are very different from my own."*
>
> —Audre Lorde, writer, feminist, librarian, and civil rights activist who confronted issues of sexism, homophobia, and racism through her writing

Affirmation Station

I am strong.

I am fearless.

No one can come between me and the power at my center.

"If you always do what interests you, then at least one person is pleased."

–Katharine Hepburn, film, television, and stage actress, a legendary leading lady in the Golden Age of Hollywood Cinema

"We must keep both our femininity and our strength."

–Rukmini Devi Arundale, dancer and choreographer of the Indian classical dance form of Bharatanatyam

"I have learned over the years that when one's mind is made up, this diminishes fear; knowing what must be done does away with fear."

–Rosa Parks, activist in the civil rights movement famous for her boycott on the Montgomery bus and known as "the first lady of civil rights"

"Once you figure out what respect tastes like, it tastes better than attention."

–Pink, singer and songwriter who has sold forty million records and won three Grammys

Affirmation Station

I am independent.
I will always take care of myself.
I will not say yes until I want to.

"I am not a woman. I am a human being."

–Indira Gandhi, politician and leader in the Indian National Congress and the first female prime minister of India

"If my art is symbolic of any one thing, it is symbolic of the freedom of woman and her emancipation."

–Isadora Duncan, dancer who performed throughout the US and Europe

"You've got to learn to leave the table when love's no longer being served."

–Nina Simone, singer, songwriter and civil rights activist who was inducted into the Rock & Roll Hall of Fame in 2018

Eva Peron

Born in the small town of Los Toldos on the Argentine Pampas,
Eva Duarte grew up in poverty, losing her father at six years
old. At the age of fifteen, she decided to travel to Buenos Aires
and pursue an acting career performing on the radio. Her voice
work attracted the attention of government candidate Col. Juan
Peron, and the two were married in 1945. He began his race for
the presidential seat in Argentina while she remained active in
the campaign, winning the hearts of citizens. Juan won the race
and accepted the role in 1946.

Without an official role, Eva Peron acted as de facto minister
of health and labor, campaigning for and granting generous
wage increases for the workers' unions within the country. She
would go on to cut off government subsidies, which made
her enemies within the more elite classes, and replaced the
subsidies with her Eva Peron Foundation, which was supported
by union and business contributions as well as other funds.
Through her foundation's resources, they were able to establish
thousands of hospitals, schools, orphanages, homes for the
elderly, and other charitable organizations.

In addition to fighting for the lower Argentine classes, Peron
was also responsible for passing the women's suffrage law and
formed the Peronista Feminist Party in 1949. Her story would

go on to inspire numerous books and other works, the most famous being the musical *Evita* by Andrew Lloyd Webber and Tim Rice, later adapted into a film starring Madonna as Peron.

Although she passed away in 1952 due to cancer at only thirty-three, Eva Peron will be remembered as someone who used her power and influence to help her nation's citizens who desperately needed it. She truly was a woman of the people.

> *"I try to remember the people who would be desperate to have all the things I take for granted."*
>
> —Rachel Clarkson, board-certified dietitian who is fascinated with science and the impact food has on our DNA

> *"I love knowing my rights and my responsibility as a child."*
>
> —Thandiwe Chama, educational rights activist in Zambia who won the International Children's Peace Prize in 2007 at the age of sixteen

Your Safe Space Is Sacred

Having one's boundaries respected can make all the difference in the world. If you are someone who grew up without a safe space, now is the time to make one: a place that is yours, one that no one can enter unless you say so. This is not silly or selfish; it is part of establishing healthy well-being as a woman in a patriarchal society.

When someone steps over the line into a place where you don't want them to be, this is an invasion of not just your physical space, but your emotional space as well. Your own individual energy is precious and is yours to give or keep as you choose. Your time? Yours to give as you see fit. Are you claustrophobic and don't want to participate in the company team-building event, which just happens to be an escape room? No explanation is necessary. Is a family member or friend always asking for hugs? That is something you are always allowed to give a hard pass when offered.

Never, ever apologize for refusing or saying no to anything—not even if it's something small, like an invitation to coffee, and certainly not if it's something bigger like a marriage proposal. You know you better than anyone else does. If something doesn't feel right, listen to that instinct. Search your soul, follow your heart, and if you want to say yes to someone or something, do it. Or say no. Either can be the right answer when it comes to you as long as it is *your* decision.

Chapter 5

HEALTHY HABITS FOR EVERY WOMAN

You Need To Care About You

We all know how incredible it feels to be the root cause of someone else's joy. As we've already talked about, doing something small for others can make a big difference. Now, the question is: Why wouldn't we apply this same principle when it comes to our own happiness?

As a badass woman, you are killing it day after day. This can be within your role in the corporate world, as a stay-at-home mom, or as a working parent who is juggling it all—and no matter what path you find yourself on, you deserve a break, and while we're at it, a treat. It's as simple as that.

Try soaking your feet, having a facial, treating yourself to dinner. Or go beyond the mundane to splurge on a real vacation—maybe with your partner or a friend, or fly solo. A change of scenery is a whole other level of self-care: It helps us truly disconnect and gain some perspective that we often very much need. Go on, give it a try. Make a commitment to pamper yourself a little on the way to realizing your dreams.

Affirmation Station

I deserve care.
I choose to put myself first.
I will treat myself.

Stop! In The Name of Love

A big part of self-care is positive reinforcement. It is essential that while we are taking care of ourselves physically, we remember to take care of our emotional needs by treating ourselves with the utmost respect at all times. This means that we must refrain from negative self-talk. You are the pinnacle of awesome and thus deserve kindness no matter what the circumstances. In short, cut yourself some slack.

The extremely wise Dawna Markova, the author of some of my favorite books, including *I Will Not Die an Unlived Life*, says, "Your soul remembers when you put yourself down; it imprints upon you. Never do this. Self-compassion is key to a life well-lived."

Many often ask, but how can I take better care of myself? You know the feeling too well: You're worn out. The end of the rope you're dangling from is frayed and about to snap. But you can't stop. Your to-do list is longer than the beginnings of that novel you've been working on, and every second that ticks by is gone forever. Stop! You're no good to anyone in this state—not to your boss, your best friends, your family, and most of all, not to yourself. When life piles on in this way, take a step back and embrace a concept that is becoming increasingly popular: mental health days.

You know your body and mind better than anyone. When you begin to crumble with everything on your plate, it's time to press pause. The best part? Your mental health day can be anything *you* want it to be. It can be a nap, a walk, reading a book, soaking in a bath, binging a show on Netflix, or maybe best of all, doing nothing. When's the last time you took a step back and really took a moment for yourself? When we do those little things for ourselves that bring us immense happiness and fulfillment, it feeds our very souls. It breathes life into our hearts and minds. We give love to those around us in a variety of ways—friendships, partnerships, family—but making sure that we ourselves don't miss out on that love is crucial.

Affirmation Station

I will say no if necessary.

I always deserve the best.

I am a hard-working woman who needs rest.

Make Your Day More Beautiful

Try out some new and positive habits to implement into your daily life:

- Be Kind to Yourself
- Live a Life of Transparency: Be Honest and Straightforward in Everything You Do
- Say No When Necessary
- Stop Apologizing
- Start Your Morning with Mindfulness
- End Your Day with Peace and Positivity

"Once I learned to like me more than others did, then I didn't have to worry about being the funniest or the most popular or the prettiest. I was the best me, and I only ever tried to be that."

—Issa Rae, actress, producer, and writer of the bestselling memoir *The Misadventures of Awkward Black Girl*

"The question is not whether we will die, but how we will live."

—Dr. Joan Borysenko, PhD, leading expert on stress, spirituality, and the mind/body connection

"Relaxation is an art that has been made very difficult to practice by the conditions of modern civilization."

—Alanis Morissette, musician, singer, and songwriter whose album *Jagged Little Pill* sold more than thirty-three million copies

"Life itself is the proper binge."

—Julia Child, cooking teacher and author who is credited for bringing French cuisine to America

"Forget inspiration. Habit is more dependable. Habit will sustain you whether you're inspired or not."

—Octavia Butler, science fiction author and winner of Hugo and Nebula awards

Affirmation Station

I choose to love myself.
I will not worry about upsetting others.
I refuse to apologize for putting myself first.

"If you can learn to love yourself and all the flaws, you can love other people so much better. And that makes you so happy."

—Kristin Chenoweth, actress and singer famous for her work on the Broadway stage

"For fast-acting relief, try slowing down."

—Lily Tomlin, actress, comedian, and writer who has performed on stage and screen for decades and has been nominated for an Oscar and multiple other awards

"The sound of birds stops the noise in my mind."

—Carly Simon, musician and writer who has recorded multiple Top 40 hit songs and authored five children's books

"Self-care is so much more than a beauty regimen or an external thing you do. It has to start within your heart to know what you need to navigate your life. A pedicure doesn't last, but meditating every day does."

–Carrie-Anne Moss, film and television actress famous for her performance as Trinity in *The Matrix* films

"Almost everything will work again if you unplug it for a few minutes, including you."

–Anne Lamott, novelist and political activist known for covering controversial topics such as religion, mental health, and substance abuse

---

Affirmation Station

I will not doubt my instincts.
I am always allowed to define my own boundaries.
I choose to allow myself an indulgence.

"You learn how to negotiate self-care and endurance over a long period of time. I was so used to doing indie movies—the filming schedule for those lasts a couple of weeks. It's easy to keep up your energy for that, because it's an exciting three weeks. That's not to say my show isn't exciting, it is, but after three months, that adrenaline is not enough. You actually have to participate in self-care to keep that energy."

—Constance Wu, actress who was voted one of *TIME*'s 100 most influential people in 2017

"It's been a lot of fun making the revolution."

—Betty Friedan, feminist writer and activist whose book *The Feminine Mystique* is often credited with sparking the second wave of American feminism in the twentieth century

Betty Friedan

When Betty Friedan submitted her article in 1956 about the frustrations women were experiencing in their traditional roles as housewife and mother, she received rejections from *McCall's*, *The Ladies' Home Journal*, and every other publication she approached. The editors, all men in that day and age, were pretty disapproving, too, going so far as to say any woman would have to be "sick" not to be completely satisfied in her rightful role!

But Friedan knew that she and millions of women like her were not sick, just stifled. She put aside her dream of being a psychologist for fear of becoming a spinster, instead choosing to marry and work for a small newspaper. She was fired from her job when she got pregnant for the second time, and began, like most middle-class women of her day and age, to devote herself full-time to the work of running a home and family, what she called "the dream of life, supposedly, of American women at that time." But after a decade of such devotion, she still wasn't happy and theorized that she wasn't alone. A graduate of Smith College, she decided to poll her fellow alumnae. Most of her classmates, who had given up promising careers to devote themselves to their families, felt incomplete; many were deeply depressed. They felt guilty for not being completely content sacrificing their individual dreams for their families, each woman certain that her dissatisfaction was a personal failing. Friedan called this "the problem that has no name," and so she gave it one: "the feminine mystique."

Over the next five years, her rejected article evolved into a book as she interviewed hundreds of women around the country. *The Feminine Mystique* explored the issue, criticizing American advertisers' exclusively domestic portrayal of women and issuing a call to action for women to say no to the housewife role and adopt a "new life plan" in which they could have both families and careers. With its publication in 1963, *The Feminine*

Mystique hit America like a thunderbolt; the publisher W.W.I. Norton had printed only 2,000 copies, never anticipating the sale of three million copies in hardcover alone!

Unintentionally, Friedan had started a revolution; she began to be flooded with letters from women saying her book had given them the courage to change their lives and pursue equal access to employment opportunities and other equality issues. Ultimately, the response to her challenge created the momentum that led to the formalization of the second wave of the US women's movement in 1966 with the organization of NOW—the National Organization for Women.

Friedan was NOW's first president and took her role as a leader in the women's movement seriously, traveling to lectures and campaigns for change and seeding many of the freedoms women now enjoy. She pushed for equal pay for equal work, equal job opportunities, and access to birth control and legalized abortion. In 1970, she quit NOW to fight for the Equal Rights Amendment, and in 1975, was named Humanist of the Year. Of her, author Barbara Seaman wrote, "Betty Friedan is to the women's movement what Martin Luther King was to Blacks."

In 1981, responding to critics who claimed feminism ignored the importance of relationships and families to most women, she penned *The Second Stage*, in which she called on men and women to work together to make both the home and the workplace havens for both genders. Before her death in 2006, Friedan was making another revolution with her book *The Fountain of Age* by raising consciousness about society's stereotypes about aging, thirty years after she, as futurist Alvin Toffler so aptly put it, "pulled the trigger of history" with *The Feminine Mystique.*

> "Meditation, yoga, working out, and eating well. That's my wellness. And I think occasionally you have to treat yourself, so if you do need to take yourself shopping, go take yourself shopping."
>
> —Cynthia Erivo, actress, singer, and songwriter who gained recognition for her work in the Broadway revival of *The Color Purple*

Affirmation Station

I will never talk down to myself.
I now recognize my innate worth.
I choose health over stress.

"Women need solitude in order to find again the true essence of themselves."

—Anne Morrow Lindbergh, author and aviator who was the first woman to receive a US glider pilot license

"Self-care doesn't necessarily mean jogging!"

—Sandra Oh, actress known for her television performances in *Grey's Anatomy* and *Killing Eve*

"I am watching, my doubts will not be subdued. [I will] commit heresy with intelligence...if my convictions compel me to do it."

—Elizabeth Blackwell, physician who was the first woman to receive a medical degree in the US

Elizabeth Blackwell

After Elizabeth Blackwell was born in England, her family moved to the United States in 1831, settling in Cincinnati when their sugar refinery in New York burned down in 1835. They were progressives, and her father, Samuel, had chosen to refine sugar from beets because it could be done without slave labor. However, the malaria-ridden Ohio River Valley soon took Samuel Blackwell's life, and the children all had to work to support the family. Musically talented Blackwell taught music classes and assisted her siblings in running a boarding house in the family home. She had a chance to teach in Kentucky but couldn't tolerate the idea of living in a slave state.

Befriended by Harriet Beecher Stowe, Blackwell became very active in the anti-slavery movement and expanded her literary interests, joining the Semi-Colon Club at Stowe's urging. She needed more intellectual stimulation than even the writing club offered, however, and spurned the attention of Cincinnati's young men in order to keep her mind clear for higher pursuits. When her father was alive, she had become accustomed to the excellent schooling and private tutors Samuel provided for his brood. Children were "thinking creatures," the elder Blackwells proclaimed. Further, they made sure that the girls were taught all the same subjects as the boys, quite a rare notion for the time.

When her friend Mary Donaldson died of what was probably uterine cancer, Blackwell knew she wanted to become a doctor. Donaldson had told Blackwell that she believed her illness would not have been fatal if her doctor had been a woman; a woman would have taken her seriously instead of dismissing her as merely suffering from "woman troubles" and emotionalism. Blackwell knew in her heart that Donaldson was right. Her long road to becoming a physician would be more difficult than she could ever know, but her unswerving dedication to reaching her goal was a testament to Elizabeth Blackwell's character.

Blackwell was turned down by no less than twenty-eight medical schools in her attempt to study medicine! Even her ultimate triumph at the age of twenty-six in finally enrolling at Geneva College in New York was handled insultingly. Pressured by Joseph Warrington, a noted doctor from Philadelphia who admired her fierce combination of smarts and pure pluck, the board at Geneva decided to give Blackwell a chance. They left the vote up to the all-male student body, who as a joke voted unanimously to let her in. Blackwell had the last laugh, however, when she outperformed the lot of jokers, graduating at the top of her class. Far from taking away from her achievement, their mockery made her victory all the sweeter. But she faced more obstacles upon graduation.

Blackwell first worked in a syphilis ward for women, where she was greeted with rancor and resentment by all the male physicians. The only other job she could get was in Paris at La Maternité hospital, interning in midwifery. Then her hopes of becoming a surgeon were dashed when she lost her left eye to disease. She also interned a year in London, where she met Florence Nightingale, forming a friendship that lasted all their lives. Blackwell fared no better in the United States when she tried to find work in her profession, finally going into private practice in New York City, where she was deluged with obscene letters and accosted on the street as a harlot and an abortionist. Her initial interest in women's health was evidenced by her opening the New York Dispensary for Poor Women and Children, a clinic where the unfortunate could receive medical attention. There, she welcomed two more women doctors— Emily Blackwell, her sister, and Marie Zakrzewska, both of whom had entered medical school with her help.

Blackwell's pioneering works are considerable: She authored a book titled *The Laws of Life*, lectured on the importance of women in medicine, organized a Civil War nursing outfit, and founded a health-inspection program run by the first African American female physician, Dr. Rebecca Cole. When she moved back to England in 1869, she added sex education and birth control to her lectures, argued against the use of animal testing, cofounded the British National Health Society, was a professor of gynecology at the brand-new School of Medicine for Women, and wrote several more books and tracts, including her autobiography, *Pioneer Work in Opening the Medical Profession to Women*. Elizabeth Blackwell died of a stroke at the age of eighty-nine, sixty-three years after she broke down the walls barring women from medicine.

"There is a part of Wonder Woman inside me and inside every woman, kind of that secret self that women share. We are all caretakers, giving birth, caring for our children and companions and loved ones."

—Lynda Carter, actress best known for portraying the character Wonder Woman as well as winning the Miss World USA pageant

---

Affirmation Station

I work hard and deserve a break.

I will take a step back.

I choose to be kind to myself.

"When I am constantly running, there is no time for being. When there is no time for being, there is no time for listening."

—Madeleine L'Engle, author of works that include fiction, nonfiction, poetry, and young adult stories, most famous for *A Wrinkle in Time*

"If you aren't good at loving yourself, you will have a difficult time loving anyone, since you'll resent the time and energy you give another person that you aren't even giving to yourself."

–Barbara De Angelis, television personality, relationship consultant, spiritual teacher, and *New York Times* bestselling author

"I want to feel my life when I'm in it."

–Meryl Streep, actress who has won multiple Oscars and other awards and is often described "the best actress of her generation"

Affirmation Station

I deserve the best.

I will strive to be healthy.

I choose to stop and take a breath.

"We can climb mountains with self-love."

–Samira Wiley, television actress known for her roles in *Orange Is the New Black* and *The Handmaid's Tale*

"When you recover or discover something that nourishes your soul and brings joy, care enough about yourself to make room for it in your life."

—Jean Shinoda Bolen, psychiatrist, Jungian analyst, women's activist, and author of thirteen books in over one hundred foreign editions

"The challenge is not to be perfect—it's to be whole."

—Jane Fonda, actress, political activist, and environmentalist known for her open and honest personality

"Invent your world. Surround yourself with people, color, sounds, and work that nourish you."

—Susan Ariel Rainbow Kennedy, author and illustrator of over sixteen self-help books that have sold more than two million copies

---

Affirmation Station

I do not owe anyone an explanation.

I am an amazing woman.

I choose to live a healthy, vibrant life.

"Self-care isn't selfish. It's self-esteem."

–Ashley Judd, actress and political activist whose career has spanned three decades

"The thing that is really hard, and really amazing, is giving up on being perfect and beginning the work of becoming yourself."

–Anna Quindlen, author and journalist who has written several novels and been awarded the Pulitzer Prize for her *New York Times* column

Faye Wattleton

Faye Wattleton was working as a student nurse at Harlem Hospital when one particular case drew her attention to the importance of safe and legal abortion. She recalls it was "a really beautiful seventeen-year-old girl. She and her mother had decided to induce an abortion by inserting a Lysol douche into her uterus. It killed her." That's when Wattleton became a reproductive rights activist, going on to hold various positions in public health administration and the Planned Parenthood Federation of America (PPFA) before being elected in 1978 to the PPFA presidency. (Ironically, she was in the process of giving birth when she won!)

She was born on July 8, 1943, in St. Louis, Missouri; her mother was a traveling preacher and her father a construction worker. While her mother was away, she spent time in the care of fellow church members, which meant they often took her from place to place throughout her childhood. At the age of sixteen, she earned her high school diploma, and she went on to attend Ohio State University, where she would receive her nursing degree.

She carries the triple honors of being the first woman, the first African American, and the youngest person ever to head up PPFA. Over the years, she has worked valiantly to fight the barriers constantly being put in the way of reproductive freedoms—from President Reagan's "squeal rule" to require notifying parents of distribution of birth control or even information to the "gag rule" preventing abortion counseling, not to mention Supreme Court challenges to Roe v. Wade. She resigned the PPFA presidency in 1992. Pointing to her contributions, Arthur J. Kopp of People for the American Way noted, "Her remarkable ability to communicate difficult issues has made her a giant in the ongoing battle to preserve Americans' fundamental liberties."

"Don't take your health for granted. Don't take your body for granted. Do something today that communicates to your body that you desire to care for it. Tomorrow is not promised."

—Jada Pinkett Smith, actress and talk-show host who owns her own television company

Affirmation Station

I will do something for myself.
I am always allowed to take a break.
I choose to be happy.

"To experience peace does not mean that your life is always blissful. It means that you are capable of tapping into a blissful state of mind amidst the normal chaos of a hectic life."

—Jill Bolte Taylor, teacher and public speaker who survived a massive stroke which inspired her to study the human brain and publish her book, *My Stroke of Insight, A Brain Scientist's Personal Journey*

Affirmation Station

As I breathe, I am filled with vitality.

I will live a healthy life.

I choose self-care.

"Every one of us needs to show how much we care for each other and, in the process, care for ourselves."

—Princess Diana, member of the British royal family whose activism and glamour made her an international icon

"Every morning, look in the mirror and affirm positive words into your life."

—Lailah Gifty Akita, author and founder of the Smart Youth Volunteers Foundation

Autumn Peltier

Teenage activist Autumn Peltier was born and raised on the shores of Lake Huron, where she attended school in Ottawa. When she was eight years old, she attended a ceremony at Serpent River First Nation in Ontario with her mother that inspired her to learn about the need to protect water sources. Contaminated water on reserves in Canada caused by pipeline leaks and pollution is an ongoing problem, and Peltier decided she wanted to do something about it, especially when she found out that the Serpent River community had been on a "boiled-water advisory" for the past ten years.

Peltier educated herself on the importance of clean water and respect for the environment, with her mother and great-aunt there to guide her in her journey. Her great-aunt Josephine Mandemin was known as the "water walker" as she was the Anishinabek Nation Chief Water Commissioner. When Josephine passed away in 2019, Peltier assumed the role.

Peltier has spoken out in front of the United Nations to project her vision of a world where everyone has access to fresh water. Her list of accomplishments is incredible for a girl of her age. At the Global Landscapes Forum, a knowledge-led platform dedicated to sustainable landscapes backed by the United Nations Environment Programme (UNEP), she has addressed world-renowned guests with huge collective influence. She even called out Prime Minister Justin Trudeau at an Assembly of First Nations meeting for breaking promises for climate change. She has spread her message for climate change across the globe at hundreds of events and was nominated for the 2019 International Children's Peace Prize. She will continue to advocate for clean water and other environmental issues, and her work has clearly made an impact: Since 2015, the Canadian government has lifted eighty-eight long-term drinking water advisories as they work toward clearing contaminated reserve water sources. She was named one of Canada's "20 People to Watch in 2020" in *Maclean's* magazine and nominated for the International Children's Peace Prize three years in a row. In 2021, Peltier was awarded the RevolutionHER Community Vision Youth Award for her work as the water commissioner.

Autumn Peltier stands as an important figure in Canada's indigenous water protection movement, fighting for the right and access to clean water across the nation.

> *"There's so much good that can come out of giving to others."*
>
> —Meghan Seney, preteen owner of a business called MegsEggs where she sells eggs to people in her community

Find Your Rhythm and Rock It

When it comes down to it, there are endless everyday practices to make our lives better. The key is to make sure they become second nature. Don't do a mani-pedi just on your birthday. Make sure you take more than just a lunch break during your workday. If you said no to something last month and want to say no again because you need very necessary you-time, toss your guilt aside! They are called habits for a specific reason: It is not a one-and-done. These are new ways of life that will help our minds, hearts, and souls flourish in all the right ways.

If the challenge of instilling healthy habits within your life seems like an impossible task, reach out to a friend or professional. Sometimes we need a strategist to help us figure out what we need when we've neglected our own desires for so long. And that's okay. As a badass female, you may think you need to be "on" twenty-four hours a day, seven days a week—that you have to be kicking ass and taking names at all times. Nothing could be further from the truth. Part of being a badass is being true to yourself and your own needs and knowing when to take a moment to stop and reflect.

We all have instincts for a reason. We know when we can push a little further and when it's time to put on the brakes. Listen to that voice and honor the request from your inner self. Your body is a beautiful instrument that needs care and compassion, so do everything you can to make sure it gets the love it very much deserves.

Chapter 6

YES, YOU CAN DO HARD THINGS!

The Future Is Female

When I was growing up, I lost count of how many times I was told by the boys on the playground that I "throw like a girl." Using gender as an insult? Simple yet diabolical. I took this patronizing phrase and let it ignite a fire within me that made me throw harder and run faster. When others underestimate us or make judgments solely based on our XX chromosome, use this as a weapon. Let it fuel you and allow it to pave your path to greatness.

In the late 1800s, a young woman named Elizabeth Cochran read an article in her local newspaper about how women were only for having children and keeping their house in order. Feeling (rightly) outraged, she wrote a rebuttal to the newspaper; in a bizarre twist, they gave her a job as a reporter. She would go on to do groundbreaking work in journalism under the pseudonym Nellie

Bly, paving the way for women in media and setting the world on fire.

This is just one example of how a woman took our society's ridiculous opinions and fought back. We all have a voice, and we all have something to say. It is time to find yours.

Affirmation Station

I can do all things.
I am graced for my race.
I am exactly where I need to be.

Nobody Puts Baby in a Corner

Throughout history, women have been kept on the sidelines, told that they were not capable or good enough and that the only things they had to offer were their appearance and their ability to produce children. Today? We can strike down those stereotypes—and we should never hesitate to do so. If there is something you want to do, what are you waiting for? Dream up a goal, make a plan, and stay present in the moment as you work it out. Most importantly, do not let anyone discourage you from stepping up to the plate and achieving that goal.

Affirmation Station

I will not be held back.
I am a woman of spirit.
I am stronger than my fear.

If You Think "I Can't," Do It Anyway

Make a list of things that you've been putting off and/or avoiding due to fear. They can be small or big things—start off with four, and try to do one per week for the next month. Write down your feelings and thoughts while tackling these seemingly impossible tasks.

"Champions keep playing until they get it right."

—Billie Jean King, tennis player who was once number one in the world, winning thirty-nine Grand Slam titles

"Women are leaders everywhere you look—from the CEO who runs a Fortune 500 company to the housewife who raises her children and heads her household. Our country was built by strong women, and we will continue to break down walls and defy stereotypes."

—Nancy Pelosi, politician who serves as the Speaker of the House of Representatives, the only woman in history to hold this position

"I've been through it all, baby. I'm mother courage."

—Elizabeth Taylor, actress during the Golden Age of Hollywood cinema, named by the American Film Institute as the seventh greatest female screen legend

"I'm tough, ambitious, and know exactly what I want."

—Madonna, singer, songwriter, and actress who has been named the "Queen of Pop"

"If particular care and attention are not paid to the ladies, we are determined to foment a rebellion, and will not hold ourselves bound by any laws in which we have no voice or representation."

—Abigail Adams, wife of second US President, John Adams, and the second First Lady of the United States

Affirmation Station

I am capable.

I am fierce.

I can do anything.

"I believe in a lively disrespect for most forms of authority."

–Rita Mae Brown, lesbian feminist writer known for her autobiographical work *Rubyfruit Jungle*

"I can, therefore I am."

–Simone Weil, philosopher, mystic, and political activist who has been described as "the only great spirit of our times"

"You can't be brave if you've only had wonderful things happen to you."

–Mary Tyler Moore, actress known for her performances in the popular sitcoms *The Dick Van Dyke Show* and *The Mary Tyler Moore Show*, which helped pave the way for more true-to-life portrayals of women in media

"And the trouble is, if you don't risk anything, you risk more."

–Erica Jong, novelist known for her written work *Fear of Flying*, which was part of a new wave of feminism

Affirmation Station

I will not let others stand in my way.

I choose to do the impossible.

I am a warrior.

"Speak up for yourself, or you'll end up a rug."

–Mae West, stage and film actress known for her unapologetic portrayals of sex symbols

"I felt that one had better die fighting against injustice than to die like a dog or rat in a trap. I had already determined to sell my life as dearly as possible if attacked. I felt if I could take one lyncher with me, this would even up the score a little bit."

–Ida B. Wells, investigative journalist, educator, and early leader in the civil rights movement

Ida B. Wells

Ida Bell Wells-Barnett was an African American journalist and advocate of women's rights, including suffrage. Though she was born a slave in 1862 in Holly Springs, Mississippi, six months later the Emancipation Proclamation freed all slaves.

Even though they were legally free citizens, her family faced racial prejudice and discrimination while living in Mississippi. Her father helped start Shaw University, and Wells received schooling there, but when she was sixteen, her parents and one of her siblings died of yellow fever. This meant that as the eldest, Wells had to stop going to school and start taking care of her eight sisters and brothers. Since the family direly needed money, Wells ingeniously convinced a county school official that she was eighteen and managed to obtain a job as a teacher. In 1882, she moved to her aunt's in Nashville, where she lived with several siblings and at last was able to continue her education at Fisk University.

A direct experience of prejudice in 1884 electrifyingly catalyzed Wells's sense of the need to advocate for justice. While traveling from Memphis to Nashville, she bought a first-class train ticket, but was outraged when the crew told her to move to the car for African Americans. Refusing, Wells was forced off the train bodily; rather than giving in and giving up, she sued the railroad in circuit court and gained a judgment forcing them to pay her $500. Sadly, the state Supreme Court later overturned the decision; but this experience motivated her to write about Southern racial politics and prejudice. Various Black publications published her articles, written under the nom-de-plume "Iola." Wells later became an owner of two papers, the *Memphis Free Speech* and the *Headlight and Free Speech*.

Besides her journalistic and publishing work, she also worked
as a teacher at one of Memphis's Black-only public schools.
She became a vocal critic of the condition of these segregated
schools. This advocacy caused her to be fired from her job
in 1891. The next year, three African American store owners
clashed with the white owner of a store nearby who felt they
were competing too successfully for local business; when the
white store owner attacked their store with several allies, the
Black store owners ended up shooting several white men while
defending their store. The three Black men were taken to jail
but never had their day in court—a lynch mob dragged them out
and murdered all three men. Moved to action by this horrible
tragedy, she started writing about the lynchings of a friend and
others and went on to do in-depth investigative reporting of
lynching in America, risking her life to do so.

While away in New York, Wells was told that her office had been
trashed by a mob and that if she ever came back to Memphis,
she would be killed. She remained in the North and published
an in-depth article on lynching for the *New York Age*, a paper
owned by a former slave; she then toured abroad, lecturing
on the issue in the hope of enlisting the support of pro-reform
whites. When she found out that Black exhibitors were banned
at the 1893 World's Columbian Exposition, she published a
pamphlet with the support and backing of famed freed slave

and abolitionist Frederick Douglass, as well as "A Red Record,"
a personal report on lynchings in America.

In 1896, Wells founded the National Association of Colored
Women; and in 1898, she took her anti-lynching campaign to
the White House and led a protest in Washington, DC, to urge
President McKinley to act. She was a founding member of the
NAACP (National Association for the Advancement of Colored
People) but later cut ties with the organization, feeling that it
wasn't sufficiently focused on taking action. Wells also worked
on behalf of all women and was a part of the National Equal
Rights League; she continuously fought for women's suffrage.
She even ran for the state senate in 1930, but the next year,
her health failed, and she died of kidney disease at the age
of sixty-eight. Wells's life is a testament to courage in the face
of danger.

> *"Failure is impossible."*
>
> —Susan B. Anthony, activist who played a crucial role in the
> Women's Suffrage Movement

> *"I have something to contribute and the time is ripe for its
> reception—something to give to the question of women."*
>
> —Clelia Duel Mosher, American physician and women's
> health advocate during the Victorian Era who spoke against
> the physical limitations placed on women

Affirmation Station

I will persevere.

I am finding new strength within.

I can achieve greatness.

"I believe you're here on Earth for a short time, and while you're here, you shouldn't forget it."

—Bea Arthur, television actress known for her role as Dorothy on *The Golden Girls* and the title role on the series *Maude*, a groundbreaking program that tackled various controversial topics and modeled female independence

"I'm the only one among you who has the balls to run for president." [said to the Black Caucus members at the Democratic convention]

—Shirley Chisholm, educator, author, and politician who became the first Black woman elected to the United States Congress

"We've chosen the path to equality, don't let them turn us around."

—Geraldine Ferraro, politician, diplomat, and attorney who served in the US House of Representatives and was the first major-party woman candidate for vice president

"Nothing in life is to be feared. It is only to be understood."

—Marie Curie, physicist and chemist who conducted pioneering research on radioactivity

Marie Curie

The scientist Albert Einstein most admired was Marie Curie; he once enthused, "[She] is, of all celebrated beings, the only one whom fame has not corrupted." During her lifetime, Marie Curie (née Marya Skłodowska) was the most famous scientist in the world, the progenitor of the atomic age. Born in Warsaw in 1867, she rose from humble beginnings as a governess in Russian-ruled Poland to become the first person ever to earn two Nobel Prizes—in medicine and in physics.

From childhood, Marya Skłodowska was known for her prodigious memory. When she was sixteen, her father, a teacher of physics and math, lost his savings, and she had to begin working, first as a teacher and later as a governess. In addition, she secretly took part in the "free university" movement, where she read in Polish to women workers, which was strictly forbidden by the Russian powers that be. She helped finance her sister Bronia's education in France, with the provision that Bronia would then help her.

Her fortunes rose when she moved to Paris in 1891 and began studying at the Sorbonne, one of the few schools to admit female service students. Three years later, she had earned two degrees in physics and mathematics and met the man she was to marry, Pierre Curie, who ran the laboratories at the Municipal School of Physics and Chemistry, where he also taught classes. Pierre made his bride welcome to pursue her studies and research independently at his lab. The list of firsts of Marie Curie goes on and on. She was the first to determine that radioactivity, a term she coined, begins inside the atom; the first woman to ever win a Nobel Prize in Physics; the first woman lecturer and first woman professor in the venerable Sorbonne's 600-year history; and finally, the first mother-Nobel Laureate of a daughter-Nobel Laureate.

Marie and Pierre Curie's discoveries revolutionized science and were the founding of modern physics. Unfortunately, the Curies both suffered from symptoms now known to have been the result of exposure to radiation. But at the time, Marie herself was on a roll. She identified two new radioactive elements in 1898, radium and polonium, which she named for her homeland. By 1900, Curie developed a hypothesis that moving particles made up the alpha rays emitted from uranium.

The dissertation Curie wrote based on her research was deemed to be the greatest contribution to science ever made by a doctoral student. Sadly, she suddenly lost her husband and lab partner to a fatal hit-and-run wagon accident. She carried on, raising her two children, teaching, and publishing her definitive treatise on radioactivity. Despite her accomplishments, Curie came under severe fire for an affair with scientist Paul Langevin, who was married at the time. The press lambasted her, claiming that being a woman scientist (and Polish at that) certainly explained her indecency. Curie fought back, stating "nothing in my acts...obliges me to feel diminished."

In 1911, she was nominated to the Academy of Sciences but lost by two votes; it was claimed that she was unrecognized because she was a woman. However, said the Academy, the real reason was that she was only forty-three and had plenty of time to wait for another vacancy; the man they had selected in her place was old and would not have another chance for the honor. During World War I, she devoted herself to the development of X-ray technology with the help of her daughter Irene. As her fame grew, she lectured around the world, receiving over 125 awards. Later, she developed the Curie Foundation in Paris, and in 1932, she helped found the Radium Institute in Warsaw, of which Bronia was the director. Marie Curie died in 1934 of leukemia caused by the radioactive materials she researched that had made her so well-known.

"I have ploughed, and planted, and gathered into barns, and no man could head me! And ain't I a woman?"

—Sojourner Truth, abolitionist and activist who was born into slavery but escaped to freedom, becoming the first Black woman to win a case against a white man

"I am in the world to change the world."

—Muriel Rukeyser, poet and political activist known for her written works on social justice, feminism, and Judaism

---

Affirmation Station

I will not be told no.
I vow to pursue every opportunity.
I can overcome anything.

"When anyone tells me I can't do something...I'm just not listening anymore."

—Florence Griffith Joyner, track and field athlete who set world records in the 1980s for the 100- and 200-meter dash

"Beware; for I am fearless, and therefore powerful."

—Mary Shelley, novelist who wrote *Frankenstein*, considered an early pioneer in science fiction writing

"There's nothing a man can do that I can't do better and in heels."

–Ginger Rogers, actress, dancer, and singer during the Golden Age of Hollywood cinema famous for performing with Fred Astaire

"If Congress refuses to listen and grant what women ask, there is but one course left then to pursue. What is there left for women to do but to become the mothers of the future government?"

–Victoria Claflin Woodhull, leader in the Women's Suffrage Movement who ran for the US Presidency in 1872

"I think one's feelings waste themselves in words; they ought all to be distilled into actions which bring results."

–Florence Nightingale, founder of modern nursing who served as a manager and trainer of nurses during the Crimean War

Affirmation Station

I am awesome.
I am invincible.
I will do what I think cannot be done.

"Life will move on. Life will not stop for you because you have pain, no. You have to move on. You have to work on everything."

–Yusra Mardini, swimmer from the country of Syria who competed in the 2016 Summer Olympics

"It isn't what we say or think that defines us but what we do."

–Jane Austen, late-eighteenth-century novelist who wrote several classic works of literature that continue to be loved today

"It took me quite a long time to develop a voice, and now that I have it, I am not going to be silent."

–Madeleine Albright, politician and diplomat who served as the US Secretary of State, the first female in history to do so

"It irritates me to be told how things have always been done.
I defy the tyranny of precedent. I cannot afford the luxury
of a closed mind. I go for anything that might improve [on]
the past."

—Clara Barton, nurse during the Civil War who founded the
American Red Cross

"Perseverance is failing nineteen times and succeeding
the twentieth."

—Dame Julie Andrews, award-winning actress and singer with
a career spanning over seven decades

Affirmation Station

I will step out of my comfort zone.

I am not going to be afraid.

I can make my dreams come true.

"But don't look at my disability as a weakness. It's made me the performer I am and the storyteller that I strive to be."

—Amanda Gorman, poet and activist as well as first person to be named the National Youth Poet Laureate, she overcame an auditory processing disorder and speech impediment as a child

"As long as I give my best, and I know I'm centered and know what I'm doing, then that's all that matters."

—Millie Bobby Brown, television actress known for her portrayal of Eleven on *Stranger Things* and currently UNICEF's youngest Goodwill Ambassador

"One person can make the difference."

—Wangari Maathai, environmental and political activist and the first African woman to win the Nobel Peace Prize

Wangari Maathai

Wangari Maathai is a remarkable woman. She set her sights on saving the farmlands, forests, and grasslands of her region, in the most politically unstable continent—Africa. To that end, she started the Green Belt Movement. "We wanted to emphasize that by cutting trees, removing vegetation, and having this soil erosion, we were literally stripping the earth of its color," she remarks.

Maathai comes from a sacred spot for all of mankind; the rural village she was born in is beside the Great Rift Valley, the birthplace of the first humans who walked upright. Many call her home the "cradle of life." Early on, she was instructed by her mother about the importance and sanctity of land and that which grows upon it, especially trees. In 1960, she left her village and took a scholarship offered to Kenyans by the United States. She found higher education to be very much in her wheelhouse, receiving a Master of Science degree from the University of Pittsburgh and a doctorate from the University of Nairobi, becoming the first woman ever to earn an advanced degree from that institution. She then went on to rack up a number of other firsts in her homeland, including becoming the University of Nairobi's first female professor, first department chair, and the first woman in the anatomy department.

Even though she enjoyed a happy marriage to a member of Kenya's Parliament, had a thriving career, and was raising three children, she still found time to become involved with women's rights. The culture of her Kikuyu background was different from that of the district in Nairobi to which her husband had been assigned. As a Kikuyu woman, Maathai had been free to express her opinions and actively involve herself in village affairs; but in Nairobi, she was regarded as much too uppity for her own good. Proving them right, she decided to run for Parliament and quit her job at the university to work full-time on her campaign. When she was then told she was ineligible to run for Parliament because she was a woman, the university refused to hire her back.

Maathai then turned her prodigious energy to the cause of ecology. On World Environment Day in 1977, she and her supporters planted seven trees in a public park, laying the foundation for the Green Belt Movement. Put down by many and even beaten with clubs as a nonviolent protester, she was accused of throwing her education and talent away. This time, she proved everybody wrong. She discovered that only 3 percent of the Kenyan forest was still standing. As a result, Kenyan villagers were suffering malnutrition, erosion of their farmland, and the subsequent loss of water as springs and creeks dried up. She quite accurately foresaw famine and environmental disaster unless trees were again planted to begin to restore the environment to its natural state. Maathai traveled throughout Kenya, teaching village women how to plant trees, including how to start seedlings from seeds they collected. Soon children got involved in the Green Belt planting projects, and by 1988, more than 10,000 trees had been planted.

Wangari Maathai's brilliant strategy is simple. She doesn't try to convert villagers to the program. She waits for word of its good work and practical results to spread; soon enough, the Green Belters would receive invitations asking them to come to another area. In addition to helping to stem the tide of the complete destruction of Kenya's ecosystem, her Green Belt Movement has provided many economic opportunities for Kenya's women.

Over the years, Maathai has received greater recognition for founding the Green Belt Movement than any parliamentary seat would have provided. She has received many awards, including a Nobel Peace Prize and a "Woman of the World" award from Diana, Princess of Wales, as well as widespread encouragement to continue her invaluable work in the regreening of Africa's precious heartland.

"Whatever women do, they must do twice as well as men to be thought half as good. Luckily, this is not difficult."

–Charlotte Whitton, the first female mayor of a major city in Canada: the capital city of Ottawa

---

Affirmation Station

I know I am able to manifest what I desire through my actions.

I believe I can.

I will not let anyone tell me I can't.

"People used to always talk down to me, like, 'Oh, you're so young,' but now I recognize that my age is an advantage; there's a lot more I can do."

–Rowan Blanchard, actress and political activist who was voted one of *TIME*'s Most Influential Teens

"The more opposition I encountered, the more I was in my element and the more caustic I became with my opponents."

–Emma Goldman, political activist and writer who played a crucial role in the development of anarchist political philosophy in the early twentieth century

Affirmation Station

I will not back down.

I am a strong woman.

I can accomplish great things.

"You can't build a reputation on what you intend to do."

—Liz Smith, gossip columnist for various publications who was known as "The Grand Dame of Dish"

"Be brave and clear. Follow your heart, and don't be overly influenced by outside factors. Be true to yourself."

—Shirley Temple, child actress, singer, dancer, and diplomat who grew up to be a United States ambassador

"Because I am a woman, I must make unusual efforts to succeed. If I fail, no one will say, 'She didn't have what it takes.' They will say, 'Women don't have what it takes.' "

—Clare Boothe Luce, author, politician, and US ambassador who wrote the hit play *The Women*, which had an all-female cast

Coretta Scott King

Like Paul Robeson and his wife, the Kings had a marriage based on love—for each other and for racial equality. After the assassination of Dr. Martin Luther King, Jr., Coretta gained recognition in her own right as a pillar of the civil rights movement.

A talented musician, King was born in Alabama in 1927 and was educated at Antioch College, where she got a degree in music and elementary education and was exposed to whites in a very different environment than the South, learning a great deal about techniques to foster interracial communication. In 1953, she married Martin Luther King, Jr., while they were both college students, and they pursued a life together, seeded by her music—she went on to earn a higher degree at the New England Conservatory of Music—and his theological degree. From a long line of ministers, Martin felt a call to become a pastor, a decision that found the young couple moving to Montgomery, Alabama, after completing their education. They had their first of four children in their first year at the Dexter Avenue Baptist Church and became deeply involved in the actions of the civil rights movement. Martin Luther King, Jr., led the bus boycott after Rosa Parks's historic bus ride. As the footage shows, Coretta was right beside Martin at every protest, fighting for the rights of all African Americans. She also participated in fundraising for the movement by giving more than thirty concerts in Europe and the United States to raise money for Martin's organization, the Southern Christian Leadership Conference.

The Kings traveled extensively in carrying out their work—to Ghana, to India, to Nigeria, and in 1964, to Norway to receive Dr. King's Nobel Peace Prize. Four years later, the world watched in horror as Martin was gunned down in Memphis, Tennessee, during a garbage workers strike.

King didn't shrink from the work at hand and led a protest in Memphis four days later with her children at her side. Her quiet dignity captured the nation; that year she was voted Woman of the Year and Most Admired Woman by college students.

From that fateful day, King stepped forward and took up the mantle of leadership in the civil rights movement, which she shared with the young Jesse Jackson. She amazed everyone with her stamina and heart as she made speech after speech and led march after march. She received innumerable awards for her tireless lifelong efforts. She founded the Martin Luther King Jr. Center for Nonviolent Change and has led the nation in new directions, organizing antiwar protests and antinuclear and antiapartheid lobbying, as well as working for increased employment opportunities for African Americans. More than

100 colleges have given her honorary doctorates. Coretta Scott King never hesitated to give herself to the struggle for freedom and justice, viewing it as both "a privilege" and "a blessing."

> *"Risk! Risk anything! Care no more for the opinion of others, for those voices. Do the hardest thing on earth for you. Act for yourself. Face the truth."*
>
> —Katherine Mansfield, writer and journalist who is considered one of the most influential authors of the modernist movement

> *"I don't think I went in with any attitude that 'Oh, oh, I'm a girl, they're not going to like my playing.' So probably that might have been my savior, because I just went in as a musician and expected to be accepted as a musician."*
>
> —Peggy Jones, pioneer of rock and roll who played rhythm guitar in Bo Diddley's band and later became known as Lady Bo

> *"I think it's very comforting for people to put me in a box, 'Oh, she's a fluffy girly-girl who likes clothes and cupcakes. Oh, but wait, she is spending her weekends doing hardware electronics.'"*
>
> —Marissa Mayer, the first female engineer at Google, who would go on to be one of only twenty women running a Fortune 500 Company

"The women of today are the thoughts of their mothers and grandmothers, embodied and made alive. They are active, capable, determined, and bound to win...millions of women dead and gone are speaking through us today."

—Matilda Joslyn Gage, writer and activist who campaigned for women's suffrage, Native American rights, and the end of slavery

"When you look at the stars and the galaxy, you feel that you are not just from any particular piece of land, but from the solar system."

—Kalpana Chawla (at her first launch), Indian-born American astronaut and engineer who was the first woman of Indian origin to go to space

Kalpana Chawla

Kalpana Chawla was born in 1962 in Kamal in the state of Punjab, India. Perhaps it was foresight that made her parents name her "Kalpana," meaning "idea" or "imagination," because while other girls her age liked playing with dolls, she preferred to draw airplanes and had an inquisitive mind.

After getting a bachelor's degree in aeronautical engineering from Punjab Engineering College, she moved to the United States in 1982, where she earned a master's in aerospace engineering at the University of Texas at Arlington in two years.

Undeterred by the Challenger space shuttle disaster in 1986, Chawla went on to earn a second master's and then a doctorate in aerospace engineering from the University of Colorado at Boulder in 1988. Later that year, she started work as a NASA scientist, researching power-lift computational fluid dynamics. She joined Overset Methods, Inc. in 1993 as a research scientist as well as the company's vice president. She was also rated as a flight instructor and held commercial pilot licenses for airplanes, gliders, and seaplanes.

When she succeeded in becoming a naturalized US citizen in 1991, Chawla had applied for the NASA Astronaut Corps; she was accepted and began training in 1995 and was soon scheduled for her first space shuttle mission, joining the six-astronaut crew of the space shuttle Columbia. The two-week mission in late 1997 circled Earth 252 times, and she was in charge of deploying a Spartan satellite using a robot arm. With that mission, Chawla had become the first Indian-born woman and the second Indian person ever to fly in space. After, she did technical work for NASA relating to the space station.

She was chosen for a second mission in 2000, but technical problems with the shuttle engine prevented it from going forward. At last she returned to space in 2003 aboard Columbia; but after a sixteen-day mission involving more than eighty experiments by the seven-astronaut crew, the shuttle, which had sustained heat shielding damage to a wing upon launch, did not survive re-entry to Earth's atmosphere, and the entire crew was lost. Chawla was posthumously awarded Congress's Space Medal of Honor; scholarships were established in her name and an asteroid was named after her, commemorating the many achievements of her forty-year life.

> *"I was able to stand on the shoulders of those women who came before me, and women who came after me were able to stand on mine."*
>
> —Christine Darden, mathematician, data analyst, and aeronautical engineer at NASA who devoted her career to researching supersonic flight and sonic booms

Hermila Galindo

Born in 1896 in the city of Lerdo, Mexico, Hermila Galindo grew up in a time when the country of Mexico was in chaos. Revolutions throughout the early 1900s created seemingly endless civil unrest, and this environment helped shape Galindo's education—she went on to attend an industrial school where she studied accounting, typing, and English.

In 1915, she founded the weekly magazine *La Mujer Moderna*, a feminist publication for women. She began to become even more involved in politics, joining a liberal club that supported presidential hopeful Venustiano Carranza. As he was impressed with her work, she was hired as his personal secretary, which was the highest political level a woman could attain in Mexico at the time. While working side by side with Carranza, she convinced him to change several oppressive laws targeting women; he enacted the 1917 Law of Family Relations (which allowed a woman to get divorced) and used his resources to submit her own proposal for women's equality to the Constituent Congress of 1917. Although she was dismissed, the fire in her burned, and she decided to run for the position of deputy in Mexico City's fifth district. She won the popular vote but came in fourth place out of twenty-six. She happily accepted defeat, stating that she had never intended to win—she had wanted to show that women were perfectly capable of running for political office.

Galindo was not only known for her progressive ideas regarding suffrage and reproductive rights, she was also radical in her thinking as she believed in free love. She wanted women to be completely liberated from the oppression of patriarchal society and the Catholic Church and their anti-feminist policies. She was articulate about women's equality in a way that not many before her had been, emphasizing that women's education must be about not only sex and birth control but also pleasure and desire, and arguing that women's sexual desires were just as strong as men's.

Galindo's endless tenacity and fearlessness regarding
equal rights for women has cemented her standing as a true
feminist icon.

Shake Up the System

Have your current circumstances have convinced you that you
aren't capable of achieving your dreams? You're not alone.
Women have often found themselves in that painful place.
Maybe you're thinking, "my kids are grown and now I want to go
back to school and get my degree." Perhaps you want to make a
career change and start your own business. Or maybe you want
to leave your current job to do some soul searching about what
lies ahead. Wherever you find yourself, it is imperative that you
remember that *you are a badass*. Nothing and no one can stop
you from accomplishing whatever it is you have set out to do.

Chapter 7

STRENGTH IN NUMBERS: FEMALE FRIENDSHIPS

Stick With Your Besties

I remember my first day of high school. I was terrified. My awkward fourteen-year-old self felt like a tadpole lost in a raging ocean. As I began to shrink into the background at freshman orientation, a girl sat down next to me, and soon enough, we began talking about nothing and everything: celebrity crushes, favorite foods, music we loved. That was twenty-three years ago, and since then, we have laughed, fought, cried, danced, and remain close friends to this day.

It's not often we meet friends at a young age and stay connected. Even in this technological age, life gets in the way. This can be due to distance, other relationships, or even tension that develops into something damaging. We need to remember that community matters, especially among women. In a world that often overlooks and underestimates us, we need to stand together and hold tight to the friends we've been gifted with.

Affirmation Station

I will be a listening ear.
I strive to always be a good friend.
I vow to stay connected to others.

Just Love, No Hate

The media has often portrayed women as being against one another. You see it everywhere—in film (*Mean Girls*, *Heathers*) and television (*Pretty Little Liars*) as well as countless songs and books. Whether it's a love triangle with two women fighting over the same man or becoming angry over something the other said or did, female friendships are viewed as fragile and fake. Women talking behind each other's backs one moment and feigning friendliness the next is something we see time and time again on multiple media platforms, or perhaps even in our own lives. But it does not have to be this way—and it shouldn't.

Why have friendships between women been shown in this negative light for so long? It lines up with years of history painting women as weak or less than. The ridiculous labels "chatty Cathy" and "gabby Gertie," not to mention the collective "clucking hens," make women out to be nothing more than giggling schoolgirls gossiping. This is an incorrect and offensive assumption. Women should not be demonized for confiding in one another. And we should not let any judgmental individuals attempt to drive a wedge between us.

Affirmation Station

I appreciate the people in my life.
I will always check in.
I will tell those I love how much I care.

Stand By Your Girl

We as women should have each other's backs, not fight with other women. It is essential that we build each other up, not tear each other down. We cannot let pettiness stand in the way of what can be an important part of our lives as women:

community. We are independent and self-reliant individuals to be sure, but connection and companionship with others can enhance our lives for the better. Friendships have proven time and time again to be a valuable asset. When a woman has a solid support system around to encourage and inspire her, she can become even more capable. Take a moment to check in with the women around you and offer them words of wisdom; it is entirely possible that they need some positive reinforcement. Even the most confident woman in the room needs an ego boost.

Feed Your Soul with Friendship

Make a list of friendship goals: reach out to a friend you've lost touch with, check in with close friends, and consider joining a new group to make new connections.

"Women that believe in each other can survive anything. Women who believe in each other create armies that will win kingdoms and wars."

—Nikita Gill, poet, writer, and social media influencer

"No person is your friend who demands your silence or denies your right to grow."

—Alice Walker, novelist, poet, and social activist who became the first African American woman to win the Pulitzer Prize for Fiction

"I have a lot of good friends and not one of them has introduced themselves by saying 'I'm a very good friend.' "

—Chelsea Handler, actress, comedian, and television host known for her deadpan humor

"Anything is possible when you have the right people there to support you."

—Misty Copeland, dancer for the American Ballet Theatre who became the first African American woman to be promoted to principal dancer in ABT history

"My girlfriends are everything to me. They celebrate with you, they cry with you, they hold you when you need to be held. They laugh with you. They're mean with you! They're always there, and it's just a priceless thing to have."

—Jennifer Lopez, singer, actress, and dancer whose work in both film and music has earned her the title of the most influential Latin entertainer in America

Affirmation Station

I will not gossip about others.

I vow to always be kind.

I am someone my friends can count on.

"Life is an ugly, awful place without a best friend."

–Sarah Dessen, bestselling author, quoted from her young adult novel *Someone Like You*

"It's the friends you can call up at 4:00 a.m. that matter."

–Marlene Dietrich, German-born American actress and singer whose career began in the Silent Film Era and was named the ninth greatest female screen legend of classic Hollywood cinema by the American Film Institute

"We will need to become savvy about how to build relationships, how to nurture growing, evolving things."

–Margaret Wheatley, writer, teacher, and speaker known for her work in creating habitable organizations and communities

"When you meet your best friend in real life, or you meet your soulmate, you just know it, and you feel it."

–Lili Reinhart, television and film actress known for her role as Betty Cooper in the series *Riverdale*, a screen adaptation of the Archie comics

---

Affirmation Station

I will not distance myself.
I will be there to give advice.
I vow to be present for those I love.

"What's really important in life? Friends, friends, and friends."

–Fannie Flagg, actress, comedian, and author of the bestselling novel *Fried Green Tomatoes*

"It's important to have strong, supportive women in your life whatever you do."

–Busy Philipps, television actress known for her roles on *Dawson's Creek*, *Freaks and Geeks,* and *Cougar Town*

"If you have two friends in your lifetime, you're lucky. If you have one good friend, you're more than lucky."

—S.E. Hinton, young adult author who wrote the classic bestseller *The Outsiders*

Fannie Lou Hamer

Fannie Lou Hamer, born on October 6, 1917, was the last child of sharecroppers James and Lou Ella Townsend in Montgomery, Mississippi. While growing up in poverty, Hamer joined her family in the cotton fields by the age of six and was only able to attend school for a few years before going back to work at age twelve. In 1944, she married and took the position of plantation timekeeper as she was the only worker who could read and write.

After attending a civil rights meeting hosted by activists James Forman and James Bevel, she became involved in the effort to register Black people to vote in 1962. At the time, a literacy test was required in order to secure the right to vote, and Hamer helped teach people so they could pass the test. One day, Fannie was on a bus with a group of fellow African American youths who were challenging the "whites only" policy at the bus terminal diner. When they were attacked by state troopers called in to deal with the "insurrection," she was hurt badly and jailed with everyone else from the bus. Her sufferings had only begun, though. Hamer was incarcerated in a cell with two Black men who were ordered to beat her with a metal spiked leather billy club. She was permanently blinded in one eye by this beating and suffered kidney damage, but she emerged with even more inner resolve to put an end to racial injustice.

In 1964, she cofounded the Mississippi Freedom Democratic Party, which challenged the local party's efforts to block Black votes. Hamer and her group attended the Democratic National Convention that year, fighting for their cause. However, when she spoke to the committee, President Johnson held a televised press conference so that she would not get any airtime. (Her speech was broadcast later.) Her steadfast efforts continued as she also helped organize Freedom Summer, which brought hundreds of college students, both Black and white, into the Deep South to help with voter registration.

Finding herself blocked in her political goals, Hamer turned to economics as a strategy, providing livestock for Black farmers to breed, raise, and slaughter. It was later that she launched the Freedom Farm Cooperative, buying up land that Black people could own and farm collectively. With others' help, she purchased land and launched businesses, eventually getting 200 units of low-income housing built.

Fannie Lou Hamer worked without stopping for many related causes: Head Start for Black schools, jobs for poor Black people, and against the Vietnam War, because she felt Black soldiers were being sent to protect rights they themselves didn't have at home. She risked her life over and over to improve the lot of her people until her death in 1977, never receiving the attention that was her due. A true unsung shero, her essential belief was, "We serve God by serving our fellow [human beings]."

> *"We need to stick together and see there's more to life than pleasing men. It's important not to cut yourself off from female friendships. I think sometimes girls get scared of other girls, but you need each other."*
>
> —Zooey Deschanel, actress, musician, and songwriter famous for her role in the television comedy *New Girl*

Affirmation Station

I will hold tight to my friendships.
I will always be there.
I am a woman who builds up other women.

"I feel there's so much pressure, especially for women, to declare what their life's going to be and what their career is, and 'Are you married yet? Are you single? But you're thirty.' And girlfriends are so important. You can have a boyfriend or husband when you're thirty, but you still need your girlfriends."

–Kristen Wiig, actress and comedian famous for her multiple personas on the critically acclaimed *Saturday Night Live*

"Constant use will not wear ragged the fabric of friendship."

–Dorothy Parker, poet and writer known for her sharp wit, who was placed on the Hollywood Blacklist due to her left-wing politics

"Well, it seems to me that the best relationships–the ones that last–are frequently the ones that are rooted in friendship."

–Gillian Anderson, actress best known for her portrayal of Dana Scully in the classic television series *The X-Files*

"It's not diamonds that are a girl's best friend, but it's your best friends who are your diamonds."

–Gina Barreca, author and humorist who has written multiple books and appeared on the television programs *The Today Show*, *CNN*, *NPR*, and *Oprah*

Margaret Atwood

On at least one occasion, prodigious writer Margaret Atwood
has mentioned the comic book fantasies she read as a child
in Ottawa as her primary influences, but she seems much
more closely aligned with the Victorians she studied in her
postgraduate work at Harvard. Born in Ottawa in 1939, she
traveled with her entomologist father into remote areas of
northern Canada and the bush of Québec. Educated at the
University of Toronto, Radcliffe, and Harvard, she knew she
wanted a career in writing by the age of sixteen and started
actively working toward her dream two years later as a student
at the University of Toronto's Victoria College. By nineteen,
she began to publish her poetry as well as articles in Victoria's
literary journal, *Acta Victoriana*.

Atwood's writing often delves into the mythic, retelling Homer's
Ulysses, for example, from the vantage point of the women
who were seduced and left behind. Her novels, including *The
Edible Woman, Surfacing, Lady Oracle, Life Before Man, The
Handmaid's Tale*, and *Alias Grace*, give voice to the silenced.
The natural world is another major theme for Atwood, as are
her unique twists on the psychological. Her published work
includes nine novels, four children's books, twenty-three
volumes of poetry, and four works of scholarship. She also is
the editor of five anthologies. A film based on *The Handmaid's*

Tale was released in 1990, and her dystopian tale of women confined to a permanent underclass has now been adapted as a famed Hulu miniseries. *The Testaments*, a sequel to *The Handmaid's Tale* set fifteen years later, was published in 2019. Her novel *Alias Grace* has been released as a Canadian miniseries to great acclaim, earning a 99 percent approval rating on the Rotten Tomatoes review site. In 2016, Atwood collaborated with illustrator Johnnie Christmas to create *Angel Catbird*, a graphic novel about a scientist who, in a way similar to the Hulk and Spiderman before him, is accidentally fused in a mutation-meld with the powers and some of the body parts of an avian and a feline.

In addition to being prolific, she is also among the most awarded writers, having received more than a hundred prizes for her excellent poetry and fiction. Moreover, she is claimed by her country of origin, Canada, as having helped to establish an identity for Canadian literature. Her work in the 1970s for Anansi Press very directly aided this cause. *Survival*, which she wrote in 1972, was an attempt at "a map" for charting Canada's writers, followed by *The Oxford Book of Canadian Verse* in 1982. Her sense of place is often a theme in her fiction and poems.

Although she does not call herself a "feminist writer," Atwood said in an interview with Penguin Books that the question that drove her while writing *The Handmaid's Tale* was, "If you were going to shove women back into the home and deprive them of all of these gains that they thought they had made, how would you do it?" (She has also stated that sales of that 1990 work jumped following the 2016 election in the United States.) Strong women rising against all odds appear again and again in her work, underlining her heroine's final words in *Surfacing*: "This above all, to refuse to be a victim."

> *"We are friends for life. When we're together, the years fall away. Isn't that what matters? To have someone who can remember with you? To have someone who remembers how far you've come?"*

—Judy Blume, bestselling author of multiple children's books that include *Superfudge* and *Are You There God? It's Me, Margaret*, as well as *Forever* and *Deenie*, which included controversial topics that pushed literary boundaries and expanded awareness of the inner lives of girls

> *"Friendship is a wildly underrated medication."*

—Anna Deavere Smith, actress known for her roles in the acclaimed television programs *The West Wing* and *Nurse Jackie*

Affirmation Station

I will be thoughtful and kind to those around me.
I strive to be approachable and friendly.
I am dependable and present for my loved ones.

"I don't know about you, but my girlfriends have been my girlfriends forever, and they're my sisters and my family."

–Elizabeth Olsen, actress who has received critical acclaim for her film performances across multiple genres

"Abandon the cultural myth that all female friendships must be bitchy, toxic, or competitive. This myth is like heels and purses–pretty but designed to slow women down."

–Roxane Gay, *New York Times* bestselling author of *The Bad Feminist* in addition to published short stories and her personal memoir *Hunger*

"The only people you can share certain things with in secret are your girlfriends."

–Shirley Knight, actress who appeared in more than fifty feature films, television films, television series, and Broadway and Off-Broadway productions in her career

"It's bullshit to think of friendship and romance as being different. They're not. They're just variations of the same love— variations of the same desire to be close."

–Rachel Cohn, young adult fiction writer of the bestseller *Gingerbread* also known for her collaboration with author David Levithan

---

Affirmation Station

I will establish a support system.

I choose to reconnect with others.

I know I can't do everything on my own.

"True friends are always together in spirit."

–L.M. Montgomery, author, quoted from her award-winning classic *Anne of Green Gables*

"You find out who your real friends are when you're involved in a scandal."

–Elizabeth Taylor, actress who rose to stardom during the Golden Age of Hollywood cinema

Affirmation Station

I value my close friendships.

I will make time for those close to me.

I want to try new things that my friends love.

"I think that it's really important to have good friends. Nowadays, you can text twenty-four hours a day and be in constant contact, but every once in a while, it's nice to just get out with your girlfriends and have fun."

–Amanda Schull, actress and former professional ballet dancer known for her lead role in the 2000 film *Center Stage* as well as other television programs

"When you feel someone else's pain and joy as powerfully as if it were your own, then you know you really love them."

–Ann Brashares, author of the bestselling young adult series *The Sisterhood of the Traveling Pants*

"Trouble is like a sieve through which we sift our acquaintances. Those too big to pass through are our friends."

–Arlene Francis, actress who appeared on film, radio, and television, including as a panelist on the game show *What's My Line?*

Esther Ibanga

Esther Ibanga is a Nigerian pastor and dedicated community organizer for peace in conflict-ridden regions who has received the Niwano Peace Prize for her advocacy of peace and unity in Jos, Nigeria.

She was born in 1961 in Kagbu, Nigeria, the seventh of ten children, eight of them girls. Both of her parents were very religious; her father was a policeman who won awards for his honesty and bravery, and her mother went on many mission trips as part of her involvement with her church. Ibanga earned a degree in business administration in 1983 from Ahmadu Bello University, and after serving the mandatory year in the National Youth Service Corps, she went to work for the Central Bank of Nigeria, where she eventually gained a position as a manager. She left the bank to become the first female church leader in the city of Jos, Nigeria, in 1995. In 2010, Pastor Ibanga founded the Women Without Walls Initiative (WoWWI) in response to the constant state of crisis in Plateau State Nigeria since 2000.

WoWWI is an NGO that includes Nigerian women from all walks of life and provides advocacy, training for women in building peace, mediation between warring parties, help for people displaced within Nigeria, assistance to the poor, empowerment of women and youth, and development projects in underprivileged areas to prevent grievances from sparking violent conflicts. Her hard work and dedication have helped restore peace between Christian and Muslim communities in Jos North, a potentially volatile flashpoint. Her approach is to empower women, both inside and outside of Nigeria, to successfully strive to advance the status of women and children of all ethnicities, religions, and political leanings—to allow women to realize themselves as "natural agents of change."

Pastor Ibanga was the leader of a march in February 2010 to the Jos government house in protest of the Dogo Nahawa ethno-religious crisis, in which many lives, including those of women and children, had been lost; more than 100,000 women dressed in black participated.

When 276 teenaged girls were kidnapped by Boko Haram terrorists from their school in Chibok, Nigeria, WoWWI joined in the Bring Back Our Girls campaign with other women leaders. Rallies crossing religious and cultural lines were held to demand that the government expedite the girls' release. Pastor Ibanga continues to campaign for the freeing of the 113 girls who are still held captive and speaks internationally on the issue.

"Our instinct is to think about the bad things happening in our lives, but at the end of the day, it's always more about the people who love you."

–Zendaya, actress and singer known for her performances in the television program *Euphoria* and the Spiderman film series

"Growing apart doesn't change the fact that for a long time we grew side by side; our roots will always be tangled. I'm glad for that."

–Ally Condie, author of the bestselling young adult series *Matched*

"Sometimes, walking with a friend, I forget the world."

–Grace Paley, author, poet, teacher, feminist, and political activist who wrote critically acclaimed collections of short stories, which were compiled in the Pulitzer Prize and National Book Award finalist *The Collected Stories* in 1994

Affirmation Station

I will honor my friends with patience and understanding.

I vow to always respect the people in my life.

I will never let pettiness get in the way of friendship.

"It takes a lot of courage to show your dreams to someone else."

—Erma Bombeck, humorist known for her syndicated newspaper humor column who also published fifteen bestselling books

"Honesty is the quality I value most in a friend. Not bluntness, but honesty with compassion."

—Brooke Shields, actress and model who has been performing for more than forty years both on television and film

"Never doubt that a small group of dedicated people can make a difference. Indeed, it is the only thing that ever has."

—Margaret Mead, cultural anthropologist during the 1960s and the 1970s

"We are each other's magnitude and bond."

—Gwendolyn Brooks, poet, author, and teacher who became the first African American to win the Pulitzer Prize

---

Affirmation Station

I will seek advice from friends who offer me guidance.

I choose to love my friends as family.

I will welcome new people into my life.

"Female friendships are important because they help define us in a particular time and place."

—Victoria Scott, young adult author of the bestselling series *Fire and Flood*

"Well, female friendships are extraordinary. They don't have to be sexual to be intense love affairs. A breakup with a female friend can be more traumatic than a breakup with a lover."

—Keira Knightley, actress well known for her character portrayals in period pieces

Edwidge Danticat

Edwidge Danticat is a Haitian American short story writer and novelist who started writing as a child in Haiti before coming to the US at age twelve to live in a Haitian neighborhood in Brooklyn, New York.

As a disoriented teenage immigrant, she found solace in literature. At Barnard College in New York City, she originally intended to study nursing, but ended up graduating with a BA in French literature before going on to earn a master's degree in creative writing from Brown University in 1993. Her master's thesis formed the basis for her novel *Breath, Eyes, Memory* (1994), which became an Oprah's Book Club selection in 1998.

Her novels include *Krik? Krak!*, *The Farming of Bones*, *The Dew Breaker*, *Create Dangerously*, and *Claire of the Sea Light*, as well as her youth fiction works *Anacaona*, *Behind the Mountains*, *Eight Days*, *The Last Mapou*, *Mama's Nightingale*, and *Untwine*. Her memoir *Brother, I'm Dying* won the National Book Critics Circle Award for autobiography in 2008. She has edited several collections of essays and authored a travel narrative, *After the Dance: A Walk-Through Carnival in Jacmel, Haiti*, which gives readers an inside look at the cultural legacy of the land of her birth. Danticat is best known for her exploration of the developing identity of Haitian immigrants, the politics of the diaspora, especially as related to the experience of women, and mother/daughter relationships. Since the publication of her first novel in 1994, she has consistently won accolades for her literary accomplishments.

> *"I know I've got the right friends because they understand when they haven't seen me for three months, and then when I do see them, it's exactly as it was before."*
>
> —Jessie J, singer and songwriter who went on to become the first British female artist to have six top-ten singles from one single studio album

> *"To be rich in friends is to be poor in nothing."*
>
> —Lillian Whiting, journalist, editor, and author of poetry and short stories

Affirmation Station

I will indulge in self-care with close friends.

I will be there for my friends whenever they need me.

I choose to always be a good friend.

"True friendship resists time, distance, and silence."

–Isabel Allende, author whose books have sold millions of copies and recipient of the Presidential Medal of Freedom in 2014

Raise A Glass With Your Girls

Here is the truth: We will all experience hardships in some form or another. This could be the end of a relationship, loss of a loved one, financial struggles–the possibilities are endless. But the common denominator in the midst of these? Your friendships. Whether you have one best friend or twenty, your support system can be a lifesaver for your heart, soul, and mind when times get tough. It is important–essential even–for independent badass women to have other independent badass women to depend on.

So celebrate your friends. Don't wait for birthdays; ordinary days become extraordinary in the company of your besties. Friendships are just like any other relationship, and they need to be nurtured and tended. Go out for coffee, brunch, drinks—have your friends over for a movie night pajama party sleepover, go camping, take trips, get lost together, and share adventures. Whatever you do, just spend as much time together as you can. While it can be hard to maintain these connections when the curveballs of life come around, try the best you can, and your friends will likely do the same. The memories you make will become bonds of friendship that strengthen over time. It really doesn't matter what you do, just so long as you do it together. And always remember that friendship is not a big thing, it is a million little things.

Chapter 8

WORDS OF WISDOM FROM TRULY GOLDEN GIRLS

A Number Does Not Define You

Ageism is something that women have been facing since the beginning of time. We were once told we had to find someone, get married, have a child, and settle down—all before we were more than barely out of our teens. Thankfully, this outdated practice is a thing of the past, but sadly, ageism is not. Women are often underestimated, ridiculed, and/or stereotyped when they reach a certain age and make major career or life decisions. (Interestingly enough, this is rarely something that men face, even on a small scale.) From day one, gender shapes your experience of the world and how the world experiences you. In the big picture, maybe the distinction between male and female is irrelevant. But in our daily lives, nothing is more crucial than whether we queue up outside the ladies' room or stride straight into the (strangely vacant!) men's.

No matter where you are in your current timeline of life, you always have the power to make a change. Just celebrated your sixty-fifth birthday and want to go back to college? Yay! This is your time. Heading back out into the dating scene after a long-term relationship or painful divorce? Everyone would like you to think it's impossible to fall in love after a certain point, but this is profoundly untrue. You are more than capable of meeting someone new. (And one possible bonus is maybe no longer having to worry about potential child-rearing as a consequence. Now that's a real timesaver for you.)

We are all women trying to make it in this world. Some of us are older than others, but we are women who have lived and have wisdom to offer one another. In other words, there's a good reason that we sometimes feel that we have more in common with some random woman just ahead of us in the grocery store line than we do with our own boyfriends or husbands.

Wherever you find yourself now, embrace your years and move forward into awesomeness.

Affirmation Station

I am comfortable in my own skin.
I will not let anything hold me back.
I can accomplish my goals.

If you have an older relative, friend, or mentor, make it a priority to have coffee with them once a month. Ask them about their life, lessons they've learned, and everything in between.

"I love to see a young girl go out and grab the world by the lapels. Life's a bitch. You've got to go out and kick ass."

—Maya Angelou, poet, memoirist, singer, and civil rights activist who published multiple works and had a career spanning decades

"Love comes when manipulation stops; when you think more about the other person than about his or her reactions to you; when you dare to reveal yourself fully; when you dare to be vulnerable."

—Dr. Joyce Brothers, psychologist, television personality, advice columnist, and writer

"Taking joy in living is a woman's best cosmetic."

–Rosalind Russell, actress, comedian, screenwriter, and singer, known for her role as fast-talking newspaper reporter Hildy Johnson opposite Cary Grant in the screwball comedy *His Girl Friday*

Affirmation Station

I am an incredible woman.

I love who I am.

I am more than capable.

"The Eskimos had fifty-two names for snow because it was important to them: There ought to be as many for love."

–Margaret Atwood, bestselling author of the critically acclaimed novel *The Handmaid's Tale*

"If love means never having to say you're sorry, then marriage means always having to say everything twice."

–Estelle Getty, actress and comedian famous for her Emmy-winning portrayal of Sophia Petrillo on the hit series *The Golden Girls*

"I am like a falling star who has finally found her place next to another in a lovely constellation, where we will sparkle in the heavens forever."

—Amy Tan, author known for her groundbreaking novel *The Joy Luck Club*

Affirmation Station

I am an intelligent woman.

I have so much to offer.

I will keep going when my path is blocked and find my way through.

"Women are the largest untapped reservoir of talent in the world."

—Hillary Clinton, politician, diplomat, and public speaker who served as the 67th United States secretary of state, United States senator, and as first lady of the United States

Betty White

Older than sliced bread (no, really!), Betty White was born in 1922 and grew up as an only child in Los Angeles. At an early age, she began acting on various radio shows before getting her big break as a "girl Friday" on the show *Hollywood on Television* with Al Jarvis before getting her own live sitcom series *Life with Elizabeth*, which was unheard of for a woman at the time. In addition, she was given her own variety show, *The Betty White Show*, where she sang, interviewed guests, and performed her own commercials. Her program reached national status, and she was informed that some Southern states threatened to stop broadcasting the show due to her featuring Arthur Duncan, an African American performer. White responded with "Tough," and proceeded to give him more airtime. She became a true pioneer of television for women during this time, earning the name "the First Lady of Television."

Using her charming wit and embracing her love of competition, she became a frequent guest on game shows such as *What's My Line?*, *To Tell the Truth*, and *Password* (which was hosted by Allen Ludden, who would later become her husband). She hosted her own game show, *Just Men!*, becoming the only woman in history to win an Emmy for hosting a game show. She began doing guest appearances on television shows such as *The Love Boat, The Carol Burnett Show, The Odd Couple*, and *Mama's Family*. It was in 1973 that television star Mary Tyler Moore asked White to be a guest on the *Mary Tyler Moore Show*, where she would go on to become series regular Sue Ann Nivens, an edgy, man-crazy homemaker who always had a snarky comeback ready. White found continued success playing the aloof and kind-hearted Rose Nyland on *The Golden Girls*, which ran for seven seasons and earned her an Emmy Award for Best Actress. The groundbreaking series was known for discussing controversial topics that included gay marriage, racism, and the erotic lives of older single women.

In the early 2000s, White began making small appearances on TV as sarcastic, sassy characters, which launched her full-scale comeback; soon enough, she was starring in the hit sitcom *Hot in Cleveland* and appearing in various romantic comedies such as *The Proposal* and *You Again*. After a Facebook campaign launched to get her on *Saturday Night Live* reached one million signatures, she agreed to host the show at the age of eighty-eight. In addition to her acting credits, she was a devoted animal advocate, serving as a trustee for the Greater Los Angeles Zoo Association, an organization that educates and helps preserve endangered species, for nearly forty years.

Betty White died peacefully in her sleep just weeks before her hundredth birthday. Her career on television and film spanned seventy years. She never let being a woman stop her from doing the thing she loved: being in front of the camera, making others laugh. Her advice for living a joyful life? "Taste every moment."

"Anyone can be passionate, but it takes real lovers to be silly."

–Rose Franken, playwright and author famous for her
Claudia stories, which were later turned into films and
play productions

Affirmation Station

I will always speak my mind.

I choose to be strong.

I will give it my all with everything I do.

---

*"Love is the difficult realization that something other than
oneself is real."*

–Iris Murdoch, novelist and philosopher best known for
her written work about good and evil, sexual relationships,
and morality

"Toughness doesn't have to come in a pinstripe suit."

–Dianne Feinstein, politician who serves as the senior United
States senator from California

"Did having to struggle so much take something out of me? Not me. Not I."

—Rita Moreno, Puerto Rican-born American actress, dancer, and singer who has had a career spanning over seven decades

Rita Moreno

Rita Moreno is one of the most accomplished actresses of our time. She is one of the few individuals who has won an EGOT: an Emmy, a Grammy, an Oscar, and a Tony Award. Her Oscar win for playing Anita in *West Side Story* was the first time a woman of Hispanic descent had won an Academy Award.

Born in Puerto Rico in 1931, she moved to America at a young age with her mother for what they hoped would be a "better life." As they set forth to make their way in New York City during the Great Depression, tensions were high due to the few jobs available; in addition, Moreno faced segregation as a Puerto Rican and had to avoid certain streets due to discrimination. Coping with this injustice at a young age often made her feel worthless, so she looked for an outlet, finding it in dance.

After dropping out of high school at fifteen years old, Moreno found jobs dancing in nightclubs to support her family. In her heart, she always wanted to be a movie star, and one day, she met with the head of MGM Studios, who called her a "Spanish Elizabeth Taylor," and she received a contract the same day. Excited and in awe, she traveled to Hollywood with her mother to start living her dream. She faced mistreatment and harassment as a Latina in the movie industry, and was often objectified and sexualized from a young age. Moreno faced countless obstacles and limitations as a woman of color, as they were presented with far fewer options for acting roles that were not embodied stereotypes. She was often cast as the "native girl" or "island girl," playing one-dimensional characters with little to no depth.

In 1967, she landed the breakthrough role that would win her the Academy Award for Best Supporting Actress, that of Anita in *West Side Story*. She proved that she could do a variety of performances, later performing on the children's show *Electric Company* (for which she won a Grammy) and *The Muppet Show*, which brought her first Emmy win; her second was for *The Rockford Files*.

In the early years of trying to make it in Hollywood, Moreno was a victim of sexual assault, which later drove her to become active in women's rights, marching in the streets for gender equality and later becoming a voice within the MeToo Movement. She was awarded the Presidential Medal of Freedom by former President George W. Bush in 2004.

Moreno went on to star in the Netflix remake of Norman Lear's sitcom *One Day At A Time* playing Lydia, a confident and carefree Cuban grandmother, specifically portraying the character as being comfortable with her sexuality despite her age. Giving a whole new meaning to coming full circle, she was cast in the 2021 film adaptation of *West Side Story*, playing the character of Valentina in the remake directed by Steven Spielberg.

In a statement about Rita Moreno by former President Barack Obama, he said the following: "Eight decades after she laid eyes on the Statue of Liberty, she continues to personify its promise that here, in America, no matter what you look like or where you come from or what your last name is, you can make it if you try."

> *"I have no patience for women who measure and weigh their love like a country doctor dispensing capsules. If a man is worth loving at all, he is worth loving generously, even recklessly."*
>
> –Marie Dressler, stage and screen actress, comedian, and early silent film and Depression-era performer who starred in the first full-length comedy film

> *"If love is the answer, could you rephrase the question?"*
>
> –Lily Tomlin, award-winning actress, comedian, and writer who has been performing for nearly fifty years

Affirmation Station

I am an incredible human being.
I will never let anyone tell me I'm not good enough.
I choose to love with my whole heart.

Lily Tomlin

Lily Tomlin stands as one of the most iconic and versatile actresses of her generation. Her range and ability to create hilarious characters as well as tug at your heartstrings proves that she is a true talent in the industry.

Growing up in Detroit, Michigan, Tomlin began performing stand-up comedy in local clubs and eventually moved to New York City, appearing on variety shows where she introduced several of her own characters, including Edith Ann, an above-average intelligent five-year-old, and Ernestine, a prickly telephone operator (the latter of which was featured on Tomlin's comedy album *This Is a Recording*, winning her a Grammy). She made her film debut in the 1975 film *Nashville*, which earned her an Academy Award nomination. Tomlin's success continued as she moved to Broadway, adding a Tony Award to her shelf for her 1991 one-woman show *The Search for Signs of Intelligent Life in the Universe* (which was written by Jane Wagner, who would eventually become Tomlin's wife in 2014). She starred in the hit comedy film *9 to 5* with Dolly Parton and Jane Fonda (two additional golden girls found within the pages of this book!), which became widely successful. Her film career continued through the '80s, '90s and 2000s, starring alongside legends such as Cher, Maggie Smith, and Dame Judi Dench. She also filmed two TV movies: *The Lily Tomlin Special* and *Lily: Sold Out*, both of which earned her an Emmy award.

In addition to her work in film, she also portrayed groundbreaking characters on television, with roles on *Will & Grace*, *The West Wing*, and *Desperate Housewives*. Tomlin reunited with her costar Fonda to star in the critically acclaimed Netflix series *Grace & Frankie*, a show about two women who find themselves lost after their husbands leave them for each other, only to become best friends and have a slew of adventures.

Tomlin has graced our screens in a variety of ways, proving that she has the ability to take on any character and make it shine.

"Hate leaves ugly scars; love leaves beautiful ones."

–Mignon McLaughlin, journalist and author of *The Neurotic's Notebook* and sequels

"The greatest science in the world, in heaven and earth, is love."

–Mother Teresa, nun and missionary honored as a saint within the Catholic Church and known for her incredible humanitarian work

"Well, love is insanity. The ancient Greeks knew that. It is the taking over of a rational and lucid mind by delusion and self-destruction. You lose yourself, you have no power over yourself, you can't even think straight."

–Marilyn French, bestselling author famous for her radical feminist works

---

Affirmation Station

I will surround myself with good people.

I reject toxic relationships.

I choose to be positive about the future.

"I have never met a person whose greatest need was anything other than real, unconditional love...there is no mistaking love. You feel it in your heart. It is the common fiber of life, the flame that heats our soul, energizes our spirit, and supplies passion to our lives."

–Elizabeth Kubler-Ross, psychiatrist and pioneer in near-death studies, and author of the international bestseller *On Death and Dying*

"Lust is temporary, romance can be nice, but love is the most important thing of all. Because without love, lust and romance will always be short-lived."

–Danielle Steel, author known for her popular romance novels that have sold over 180 copies

"Romance is the glamour which turns the dust of everyday life into a golden haze."

–Elinor Glyn, novelist and scriptwriter who specialized in romantic fiction (considered scandalous at the time)

Affirmation Station

I will love who I love.

I am amazing in every way.

I embrace all of my imperfections.

"Where there is great love, there are always miracles."

—Willa Cather, award-winning writer known for her novels about life on the Great Plains

"Every individual matters and has a role to play in this life on Earth. The chimpanzees teach us that it is not only human but also non-human beings who matter in the scheme of things."

—Jane Goodall, primatologist and anthropologist who conducted groundbreaking scientific research

Jane Goodall

Born in 1934, English zoologist Jane Goodall owes her career to the fact that her divorced mother couldn't afford to send her to college. Instead, the amateur naturalist worked in offices and waitressed in order to pay for travel to feed her great curiosity. In 1960, she received an invitation to visit a friend whose family had moved to Kenya. While there, the young woman worked up the nerve to contact Louis and Mary Leakey, who were working there to find evidence of early humans in the Olduvai Gorge in the Great Rift. The Leakeys found her to be an able companion, well suited to working in the field looking for fossil fragments or at Kenya's National Museum of Natural History, reconstructing what they found. Despite the fact that she had no formal scientific training, Dr. Louis Leakey asked her to go to Tanzania to conduct a lengthy study of chimpanzees in the wild.

He believed that by studying chimpanzees, we stand to learn much about the life of early humans.

Goodall, who was much more interested in animals than in Stone Age ancestors, jumped at the chance—this would be the first such long-term study of this animal in its natural habitat. When the African government refused to allow her to work alone in the animal refuge, her mother offered to accompany her. Despite her lack of training, Goodall was well suited to the task of scientific observation; she kept meticulous notes and went to great lengths to find chimps, hiking miles into the forest each day. Goodall's work was the stuff of scientific revolution.

She disproved many erroneous beliefs about chimpanzees. For example, she learned that they are omnivores, not vegetarian, and that they make and use tools, have elaborate social structures and a variety of humanlike emotions, and give their young unconditional affection. She has been decried by stuffy male zoologists for giving the chimps names like "Graybeard" instead of numbers in her papers. Goodall did it "her way" and outdid all the uptight academics with her commitment, endurance, and plain smarts. In many ways, she received better treatment from her subjects than her peers, especially in the heartwarming moment when a male chimpanzee accepted a nut from her hand, clasping her hand soulfully before discarding the nut. Goodall was touched at his attempt to spare her feelings about the unwanted nut.

In 1964, Goodall met and married a young photographer who came to her camp to take photos of the chimps, and they had a son. She went on to earn a PhD in ethnology from Cambridge (one of the only people ever to receive one without a BA!), and her findings have been widely published. Returning to Africa in 1965, she founded the Gombe Stream Research Centre, which has engaged in decades of continuous research in Gombe National Park. In recent years, her work has taken a slightly different turn, however, toward protecting the chimpanzees she studied and befriended in Africa through the Chimpanzee Guardian Project. She lectures around the world to raise money to try and stop the continued shrinking of their habitat and their decline in numbers from more than 10,000 during the time of her study to less than 3,000 today.

The author of many books and the winner of a multitude of awards, Jane Goodall pursues her interests with singular purpose and passion. In a realm where money and education are usually the deciding factors, she started with nothing but her natural intelligence and an open, curious mind. She went on to achieve major recognition in her field and become one of the most beloved figures in science today.

"You yourself, as much as anybody in the entire universe, deserve your love and affection."

–Sharon Salzberg, *New York Times* bestselling author and teacher of Buddhist meditation practices

"I have a reputation for being cold and aloof, but I'm so not that woman. I'm passionate. I love my girls, being with my girlfriends, getting involved with issues that affect other women and children who are suffering."

–Annie Lennox, singer-songwriter, political activist, and philanthropist who was lead singer of the successful 1980s band Eurythmics

"Some people think it's holding on that makes one strong; sometimes it's letting go."

–Sylvia Robinson, singer and record producer who later became founder and CEO of the hip hop label Sugar Hill Records

---

Affirmation Station

I strive to be a better person.
I vow to always try my best.
I am grateful for what I have.

"Just don't give up on trying to do what you really want to do. Where there is love and inspiration, I don't think you can go wrong."

—Ella Fitzgerald, jazz singer sometimes referred to as the "First Lady of Song"

"Find out who you are and do it on purpose."

—Dolly Parton, singer-songwriter, actress, and businesswoman who stands as an icon in the country music industry

Dolly Parton

Born one of twelve children in the rural Great Smoky Mountains of Tennessee, Dolly Parton is now a phenomenon in the music industry and one of the few people to have been nominated for an award in every category: Emmy, Grammy, Tony, and Oscar.

Music was in her roots from the very beginning. Growing up singing with her family in church, she landed her first singing gig at the age of ten when her uncle bought her a guitar and booked her an appearance on a local variety show. The next few years brought little success, so she packed a bag and left for the larger city of Nashville to find stardom. In 1966, two of her songs made the Top Ten, and soon enough her song "Dumb Blonde" became a Top 40 hit (a song which was an incredible ballad for empowerment that spoke up against female stereotypes).

Parton landed her big break when she was selected to appear on *The Porter Wagoner Show,* and she eventually went on to sing side by side with Wagoner as his partner. This led to a record deal and soon enough, all of her songs were hitting number one, including "Jolene," "I Will Always Love You," and "Love Is Like a Butterfly."

As the years went on and her success grew, she used inspiration from her upbringing to fuel her creativity, singing songs about living life in a small town and wanting to achieve her dreams. As she told *Rolling Stone* in 1977, "I wanted to be free. I had my songs to sing; I had an ambition and it burned inside me. It was something I knew would take me out of the mountains. I knew I could see worlds beyond the Smoky Mountains."

In addition to her success in the music industry, she landed movie roles in hit films such as *9 to 5* with Jane Fonda and Lily Tomlin, and *Steel Magnolias* with Julia Roberts and Sally Field. In 1992, her hit song "I Will Always Love You" was covered by Whitney Houston and featured in the blockbuster film *The Bodyguard*.

In 1985, she expanded her career beyond music and film by opening her own theme park in the state of Tennessee; Dollywood remains a top tourist attraction. Through all her success, prosperity, and fame, she never forgot where she came from: Parton started the nonprofit Dollywood Foundation, which has given back to her hometown's economy and provided scholarships to high school students. She started an incredible literary program called Imagination Library which gives one free book a month to children from the time they are born to the age of five; the number of books Imagination Library has put in the hands of small children exceeds 100 million, and the project has expanded across the US and beyond to countries around the world. In 2004, she was awarded the Living Legend Award by the Library of Congress. She also contributed $1 million toward research funding for COVID-19 vaccinations.

Dolly Parton has proved to everyone that humble beginnings can be the start of something extraordinary. Her story is one for the ages as she continues to sing for sold-out crowds and use her success to do great things for those in need.

Affirmation Station

I choose to go on regardless of fearful feelings.
I will speak my mind.
I am capable of the impossible.

"Love makes your soul crawl out from its hiding place."

—Zora Neale Hurston, author, anthropologist, and filmmaker known for her novel *Their Eyes Were Watching God*

"I can trust my friends. These people force me to examine myself and encourage me to grow."

—Cher, singer and actress who is known for her groundbreaking performances showcasing her sexuality and style

"A charming woman doesn't follow the crowd. She is herself."

—Loretta Young, Academy Award-winning actress who had a long and varied career in film from 1917 to 1953

Cicely Tyson

Growing up as the daughter of immigrants from the Caribbean island of Nevis, Cicely Tyson spent her early years in the New York neighborhood of Harlem. She got her start in the entertainment industry through modeling after being discovered by *Ebony* magazine. From there, she took to Broadway, acting in several shows as well as in supporting roles in films through the 1950s.

As she was determined to portray only positive images of
Black women, Tyson had limited opportunities presented to
her when it came to film and television. Nevertheless, she was
inducted into the Black Filmmakers Hall of Fame in 1977. She
went on to star in the critically acclaimed film *Sounder*, which
earned her an Academy Award nomination. From there, she
found the role that would skyrocket her to household-name
fame: the lead in the drama series *The Autobiography of Miss
Jane Pittman*, playing a 110-year-old woman whose life as a
slave in childhood up through Emancipation Day and on to the
civil rights movement is chronicled in flashbacks throughout.
This powerful performance by Tyson was recognized with
two Emmys. During this time, she was married to famous jazz
musician Miles Davis (they divorced in 1988). She also found
roles on the big screen, appearing in the groundbreaking films
Fried Green Tomatoes and *The Help*, as well as in several Tyler
Perry film projects.

She continued to star in various miniseries and television
programs through the years, including *Roots, House of Cards*,
and *How To Get Away With Murder*.

In addition to her acting credits, Tyson has been honored by
the Congress of Racial Equality, the NAACP, and the National
Council of Negro Women. She was named a Kennedy Center
honoree in 2015 and awarded the Presidential Medal of

Freedom in 2016. Her memoir, *Just As I Am*, was released in 2021, just two days before her death at ninety-six after a long and full life.

Tyson will be remembered as a powerhouse woman who never compromised or cut corners. Her incredible talent as well as her dedication to her fellow women distinguished her as an absolutely remarkable human being, truly one for the ages.

> *"Love is a game that two can play and both win."*
>
> –Eva Gabor, actress, businesswoman, singer, talk-show host, and socialite remembered for voice work in the Disney films *The Aristocats, The Rescuers*, and *The Rescuers Down Under* as well as for costarring in *Green Acres*

> *"Love and magic have a great deal in common. They enrich the soul and delight the heart…and they both take practice."*
>
> –Nora Roberts, bestselling author of more than 225 romance novels

---

Affirmation Station

I will be careful with my heart.

I vow to be true to myself.

I am a wonderful woman who deserves love.

> *"I have learned not to worry about love, but to honor its coming with all my heart."*

—Alice Walker, novelist, short story writer, poet, and social activist who was awarded the Pulitzer Prize for fiction for her novel *The Color Purple*, the first African American woman to win this top writing award

> *"Love is a fire. But whether it is going to warm your heart or burn down your house, you can never tell."*

—Joan Crawford, actress who rose to fame in the Depression era to become one of the most prominent actresses in Hollywood

Carol Burnett

Carol Burnett has established herself as one of the funniest women of the century for her performances spanning the decades from the 1960s until today.

Growing up in the Great Depression, Burnett spent her younger years in movie theaters, which inspired her to pursue acting. She attended UCLA, where a benefactor saw her perform on stage and loaned her money to move to New York City so she could keep making people laugh on a larger scale. She guest starred on various television shows before landing the Broadway hit *Once Upon a Mattress*, which earned Burnett her first Tony Award nomination.

By this time, she had proved her talent for doing all sorts of comedy, focusing primarily on slapstick. In 1967, she was given her own variety show, *The Carol Burnett Show*, which become a massive hit and ran on television for twelve years—highly unusual for a variety show at that time. The show featured famous comedy stars such as Tim Conway and Vicky Lawrence, and included performances ranging from musical numbers to comedy sketches featuring beloved recurring characters.

Burnett continued to appear in films through the '70s and '80s, notably including the musical *Annie*, as the villain Mrs. Hannigan. She continued to appear in numerous TV movies and shows such as *Magnum P.I.*, *Mad About You*, *Desperate Housewives*, and *Glee*. In addition, she cohosted the series *A Little Help with Carol Burnett*, in which children offer advice. Burnett also voiced the character Chairol Burnett in the animated film *Toy Story 4*.

In 2013, Burnett was awarded the Kennedy Center's Mark Twain Prize for American Humor, and in 2019, she became the inaugural recipient of the Golden Globes Carol Burnett Award for lifetime achievement in television.

At eighty-nine years young, Burnett has been making us laugh for nearly seventy years and shows no sign of stopping.

Affirmation Station

I choose to be courageous.

I will not let anything stand in my way.

I am someone who will go after what she wants.

"If you have love in your life, it can make up for a great many things you lack. If you don't have it, no matter what else there is, it's not enough."

—Ann Landers, advice columnist who wrote the "Ask Ann Landers" column that ran in print for forty-seven years

"An archaeologist is the best husband a woman can have. The older she gets, the more interested he is in her."

—Agatha Christie, writer known for her sixty-six detective novels and fourteen short story collections

Marla Gibbs

Marla Gibbs was working for United Airlines when she decided to pursue acting. She was forty-four when she auditioned (with just a few acting classes under her belt) for a sitcom called

The Jeffersons, set to be a spinoff of the hit comedy series
All in the Family. She landed the role of Florence Johnston, a
housekeeper to a Black family living in the Upper West Side of
New York City. Like its predecessor, also created by Norman
Lear, the sitcom was known for its progressive topics and sharp
humor. Gibbs's banter with lead character George Jefferson
quickly established her as one of most beloved characters on
television. (Even after landing this role, she continued to work
at United as a reservations agent, unsure if the role was going
to be permanent.) Showrunner Lear quickly fell in love with how
Gibbs chose to portray Florence, modeling the role after her
own grandmother and aunt—and Gibbs and Lear remain friends
to this day. Similar to *All in the Family*, *The Jeffersons* was known
for breakthroughs in social norms, such as having an interracial
married couple.

They would work together again on another sitcom: *227*,
where Gibbs played a sharp-tongued housewife. Originally
produced by Gibbs as a stage play, she would go on to sell the
rights to Lear and turn it into a hit series after *The Jeffersons* was
unexpectedly canceled after eleven seasons on air.

At ninety (which she describes as turning thirty for a third
time!), she is still gracing our screens, appearing on the soap
opera *Days of Our Lives*. In 2021, she was awarded a star on
the Hollywood Walk of Fame, and not long after, released her

memoir, *It's Not Too Late*. When asked what the title meant, she says: "I really got it from a lady that came up to me and said, 'Ms. Gibbs, I always wanted to act. You think it's too late?' I said, 'Are you still breathing? If you're still breathing, it's not too late.'"

Gibbs stands out as a bona fide shero who never let anything keep her from achieving her dreams—a true inspiration.

Affirmation Station

I will accept change.
I am capable of learning new things.
I have something of value to offer.

"All love shifts and changes. I don't know if you can be wholeheartedly in love all the time."

—Dame Julie Andrews, actress and singer who has had a seventy-five-year career and won numerous awards, including two Emmys, three Grammys, six Golden Globes, and an Academy Award

"If it is your time, love will track you down like a cruise missile."

—Lynda Barry, cartoonist, author, and teacher best known for her weekly comic strip *Ernie Pook's Comeek*

*"What the world really needs is more love and
less paperwork."*

–Pearl Bailey, actress and singer who received a special
Tony Award for the title role in the all-Black production of
Hello, Dolly!

Jane Fonda

Born into a family already famous in the acting world, Jane
Fonda grew up in New York, and after her second year in
college, she decided to leave to pursue an acting career.
She began studying in the Actors Studio in New York City,
eventually landing roles on Broadway and in small films.

Her career grew exponentially from there: Through the 1970s,
she starred in multiple motion pictures, receiving two Academy
Awards for her performances in the films *Klute* and *Coming
Home*. Throughout the decade, she was involved in several
political causes, traveling to Hanoi in 1972 to protest the
Vietnam War, which earned her the nickname "Hanoi Jane"
among hawkish proponents of that US intervention in Southeast
Asia. The following decade, she created an exercise program in
order to be able to fund Campaign for Economic Democracy,
an organization founded by Tom Hayden, who Fonda was
married to until 1990. Never one to shy away from a soapbox,

Fonda has always been active and outspoken both when it comes to women's rights and to climate change.

In 1980, Fonda starred opposite icons Dolly Parton and Lily Tomlin in the hit comedy *9 to 5*, and went on to star alongside her father Henry Fonda and acting legend Katherine Hepburn in the film *On Golden Pond*.

After taking a hiatus from acting, Fonda reemerged in the early 2000s, appearing in a run of romantic comedies and returning to the Broadway stage. She reunited with costar Tomlin in the hit Netflix series *Grace and Frankie*.

In 2021, she was awarded the Cecil B. DeMIlle Award for Lifetime Achievement. Fonda has also written several books, including the autobiography *My Life So Far*; *Prime Time*, a volume of advice about aging; and *What Can I Do?: My Path from Climate Despair to Action*. The documentary *Jane Fonda in Five Acts* also chronicled her life and career.

At eighty-five years young, Fonda has proven herself to be a trailblazer in every aspect: on film, television, and the Broadway stage, as well as off-screen when it comes to working to bring about positive change in the world.

Affirmation Station

I am a wise woman.

I will surround myself with positivity.

I choose to always be the best version of myself.

"Love is not enough. It must be the foundation, the cornerstone—but not the complete structure. It is much too pliable, too yielding."

—Bette Davis, iconic actress during the Golden Age of Cinema who was known for playing every type of character

"To live in this world,

you must be able

to do three things:

to love what is mortal;

to hold it

against your bones knowing

your own life depends on it;

and, when the time comes to let it go,

to let it go."

—Mary Oliver, poet who won both the National Book Award and the Pulitzer Prize, known for her nature-inspired work [excerpted from *In Blackwater Woods*]

One Life to Live

Time is something humans will always be chasing. We always want more of it or want to go back and do things differently. Until science fiction becomes a reality, we are all on the same clock.

You get one heart, one soul, one chance to be the best badass female you can possibly be. Break the glass ceiling. Give back. Fall in love. Raise amazing kids (only if one wants to, of course.) And when you do reach that age where things start to slow down, maybe that is the time to reflect and understand who you truly are. Perhaps it means pursuing a new passion, changing your look, or traveling the world.

If you are a young woman, talk to the older women in your life. Watch and learn from them about ways you can improve your life. If you are a woman who has lived a life as you chose, keep rocking it. Take your incredibly powerful mind and share it with others in whatever way feels right to you. Live—without fear, regret, or uncertainty.

Stay Golden

From the original Golden Girls, here is an everyday mantra:

Live like Rose.
Dress like Blanche.
Think like Dorothy.
Speak like Sophia.

CONCLUSION

Take the words spoken throughout this book and harness them. Let them be your shield in the fight against the holdovers of patriarchy. You are free to use these words of wisdom in whatever way is right for you—just make sure to go at your own pace. Maybe you need to work up to saying no to things, or yes to invoking more healthy habits. Perhaps you need to do some serious work on loving your body. In whatever manner you are working on yourself, remember that you are amazing. Do not let anyone or anything stand in your way of taking this journey toward a better you.

Be Positively Badass.

CALL TO ACTION

Dear Reader,

Writing this book was a challenge simply because it was nearly impossible to choose between the countless badass women throughout history who should be honored within these pages. Although we stand behind our countless hours of research, we would love to hear from you all with your nominations of your favorite Badass Women. It is vital that we call attention to these amazing females who didn't make it into the history books—UNTIL NOW! In addition, we as women can always use encouragement, and if you have an affirmation that fills your life with joy and positivity, tell us! (You can never have too many affirmations, after all.)

Below is a simple nomination form, and we would love to credit you, so please include your contact information. Thanks for your participation—you are pretty badass, yourself!

xoxo
Becca

I Nominate the Following Badass Woman or Women:

_____

_____

_____

_____

_____

My Personal Affirmation:

_____

_____

_____

_____

Mango Publishing, 2850 Douglas Road, 4th Floor
Coral Gables, Florida 33134
Email: info@Mango.bz

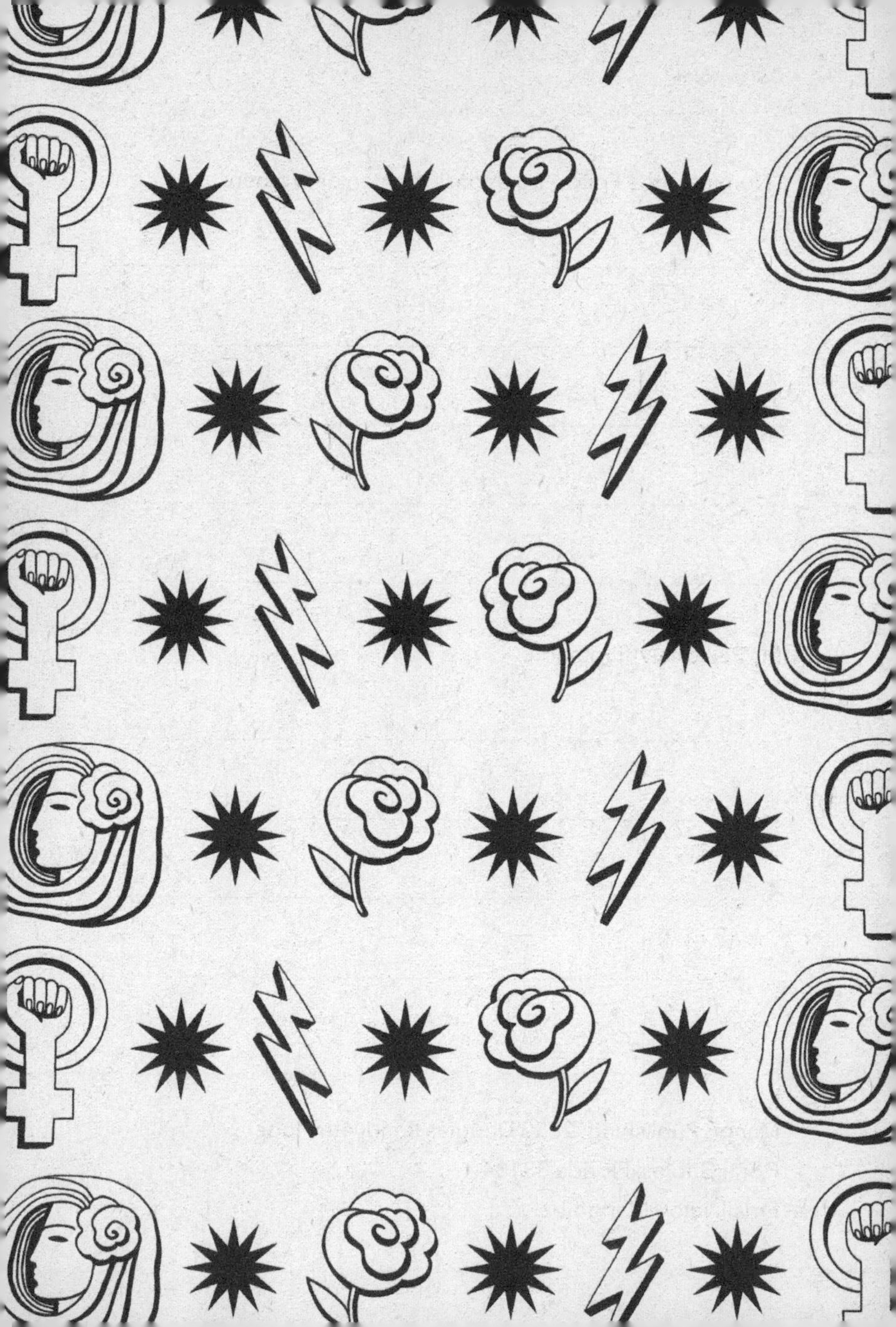

ABOUT THE AUTHOR

Becca Anderson comes from a long line of preachers and teachers from Ohio and Kentucky. The teacher side of her family led her to become a woman's studies scholar and the author of *The Book of Awesome Women*. An avid collector of meditations, prayers, and blessings, she helps run a "Gratitude and Grace Circle" virtual circle that meets weekly. In nonpandemic times, she gives gratitude workshops at churches and bookstores in the San Francisco Bay Area, where she currently resides. Becca Anderson credits her spiritual practice with helping her recover from cancer and wants to share this healing wisdom with anyone who is facing difficulty in their life.

Mango Publishing, established in 2014, publishes an eclectic list of books by diverse authors—both new and established voices—on topics ranging from business, personal growth, women's empowerment, LGBTQ+ studies, health, and spirituality to history, popular culture, time management, decluttering, lifestyle, mental wellness, aging, and sustainable living. We were recently named 2019 *and* 2020's #1 fastest-growing independent publisher by *Publishers Weekly*. Our success is driven by our main goal, which is to publish high-quality books that will entertain readers as well as make a positive difference in their lives.

Our readers are our most important resource; we value your input, suggestions, and ideas. We'd love to hear from you—after all, we are publishing books for you!

Please stay in touch with us and follow us at:

Facebook: Mango Publishing
Twitter: @MangoPublishing
Instagram: @MangoPublishing
LinkedIn: Mango Publishing
Pinterest: Mango Publishing
Newsletter: mangopublishinggroup.com/newsletter

Join us on Mango's journey to reinvent publishing, one book at a time.

CPSIA information can be obtained
at www.ICGtesting.com
Printed in the USA
LVHW022035210922
728756LV00003B/16

9 781684 810017